AMERICA
AT
WAR!

**BATTLES
THAT
TURNED
THE TIDE**

Brian Black

SCHOLASTIC INC.
New York Toronto London Auckland Sydney

*This book is dedicated to the hope
for a peaceful future.*

ISBN 0-590-45505-2

12 11 10 9 8 7 6 5 4 3 2 1   2 3 4 5 6 7/9

Printed in the U.S.A.   40

First Scholastic printing, December 1992

Contents

Introduction

*There is no truer patriot
than someone who is willing to give
their lives for their country.*

The United States was founded on the principle that every individual should have the freedom to make his or her own decisions. The United States has fought many battles in order to preserve this freedom. Some people believe that this violent history is not something to be proud of. But as President Bush told Americans in 1990, "some things are worth fighting for."

Today, the United States is the most respected military power in the world. There have been many wars that have helped the United States arrive at this point. Each war, in turn, had many battles. Some went well, others were failures. But each was filled with the courageous efforts of American soldiers.

1

After a war, each battle and each soldier becomes part of American history. As historians look back at these wars, certain battles are perceived as the turning points of a war. As in football, baseball, soccer, basketball, or any sport there is usually one confrontation, or one last push, that turns the tide. This book tells the stories of the battles that turned the tides of war, and changed American history.

The Revolutionary War
THE BATTLE OF SARATOGA

The portly seventy-year-old man looked out from behind his small, round spectacles. The window of his study in Passy, France, overlooked gardens. But his mind was not on the flowers and plants below. He had arrived from the colonies in America just under one year earlier — in November of 1776. While his countrymen were fighting the British on the battlefields, he was fighting his own battle.

He had been happy when his fellow Continental congressmen voted for him to head the American delegation to France. "I am old and good for nothing," he had shrugged. Benjamin Franklin would go on to become one of the greatest Americans who ever lived. He had many accomplishments, but it was during this trip to France that he forever put his mark on American history.

In France, this "old and worthless" man was responsible for America winning the Revolution-

Benjamin Franklin

ary War. Benjamin Franklin knew that, without help from France, the colonists would not be able to last in their war with the British. The French were interested in aiding the colonists. If Great Britain could be defeated, France would become a more significant power in Europe. But the French didn't truly believe that the American rebels had a chance. Franklin's job was to convince them that the Americans could win. But the early results of the war were making him look like a liar.

The colonists had gotten used to a great deal of freedom during the mid-1700's. Around 1763, Great Britain decided that it needed more money from its colonies. The British Parliament voted to enact new taxes on colonists, such as the Stamp Tax. The colonists hated paying these new taxes.

Worse, the colonists were given no representation in the British Parliament to argue their points. Many colonists decided to find other ways to get Great Britain to listen to them.

Groups of colonists boycotted British goods, burned the stamps, and dumped tea into Boston Harbor. Fearful British leaders sent over more soldiers. On April 19, 1775, a company of colonial soldiers, minutemen, in Lexington, Massachusetts, watched as a force of British troops approached. They wondered whether the British were coming to capture the guns and ammunition stored there. If so, they could not let this happen. Suddenly, a shot rang out — "the shot heard 'round the world," as it was later named. No one ever found out who fired that shot. But it didn't matter, the war had begun. The minutemen drove the redcoats back to Boston, where their leader sent word back to England for reinforcements.

In May, 1775, the colonies assembled the Second Continental Congress in Philadelphia. They set up their own army, under the direction of George Washington of Virginia. All together, the Revolutionary War would last eight years. The colonists suffered heavy losses in the first year. Few believed they had a chance to defeat the well-trained redcoats. Not every American even supported the revolution! Why should other countries?

Americans who refused to turn against their mother country were called Loyalists or Tories. Neutralists or Patriots were the names for the rebels who believed war with Britain was the only answer. When the war was going poorly, there were times when many Americans — Loyalists and Patriots — wished the fighting had never started.

Countries such as Spain and France had all but given up hope of any American success. It was in this situation that Franklin was called from his window in France on December 4, 1777. A message had arrived from America. Before the messenger could even get out of his carriage, Franklin was on him. "Sir," he begged, "*is* Philadelphia taken?" He was referring to the U.S. capital at that time. "It is, sir," responded the messenger. Franklin turned away in terror. "But," continued the messenger, "I have greater news than that." Greater than the American capital being taken? Franklin wondered what could possibly be greater. As he listened to the news of fighting in the northern United States, Benjamin Franklin knew this was the news he and the French had been waiting for.

It is unthinkable today to consider America being invaded by another country. But in 1776, the United States wasn't invaded by just any country — the British believed they were the owners of this vast land. They wanted to make quick work of putting down the colonists' uprising. Fighting took place in and around New York City in the summer and fall of 1776. These skirmishes were short-lasting battles. Each side needed to see what the other was made of.

During the winter of 1776, Britain drew up its master plan to defeat the colonists. It would begin in early 1777. The leader chosen to head this assault was General John "Gentleman Johnny" Burgoyne. At that time in Great Britain and other countries, many officers ruled by fear — often whipping soldiers. Gentleman Johnny tried to win the loyalty of his troops by treating them like human beings. Gentleman Johnny was equally skilled in handling a sword, speaking before Parliament, or writing a play. His troops loved him, and his opponents admired him.

To help fight the colonists, Great Britain had hired Native American and German soldiers. Burgoyne's plan called for these groups to team with British and Canadian troops. The main thrust would be an invasion from the north — from Canada. Burgoyne would lead these troops to the American stronghold at Fort Ticonderoga, New York. Once overtaken, these troops would continue to move south. At this point, General William Howe would lead his British troops from Rhode Island up the Hudson to Albany. Here, the two invasion forces would meet, trapping the American forces. The operation would separate the Americans in New England from their compatriots in Philadelphia. If accomplished, it would signal the beginning of the end for the Americans.

The British felt that their redcoated army was the best in the world. The redcoats were known for their awesome firepower. Opponents were usually allowed to come quite close before the red-

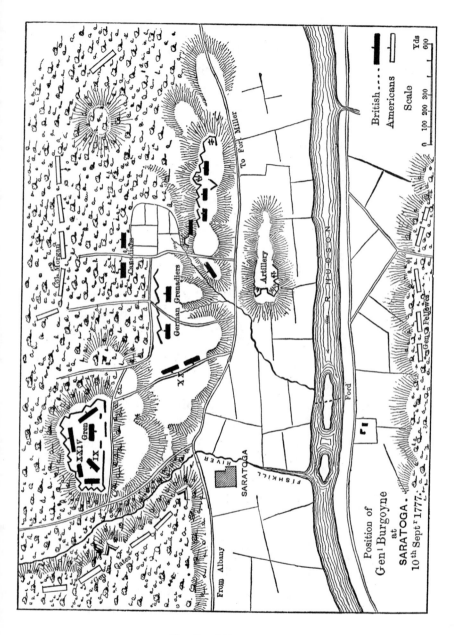

Battle of Saratoga

coats pulled their triggers. They were not accurate marksmen. But when the redcoats stood shoulder to shoulder, two or three deep, and shot all at once, they would hit anything in their path. At the order of, "FIRE!" the air would be filled with cast-iron balls each about the size of a grape. During the Revolutionary War the British used a credo that you can still hear today: "Don't fire," their officers would say, "until you see the whites of their eyes."

The colonists, on the other hand, were a rough-and-tumble group of scraggly looking soldiers. Unlike the redcoats, their claim to fame was their marksmanship. Because they all needed to hunt for their food, they had learned to be excellent shots. The Americans used a German-model rifle. Unlike the shorter and fatter British musket, these rifles were long and thin and shot further. The inside of the barrels were ridged to give the ball that was shot a spinning motion that caused it to travel straighter. This allowed the Americans to stay in their familiar woods for protection. The redcoats thought it quite unfair that the Americans refused to come out, line up, and "fight like men."

Burgoyne's troops numbered 3,724 British, 3,016 Germans, about 250 Canadians, and somewhere around 400 Native Americans. The force's only weakness was its lack of transportation. The soldiers had to travel great distances, and in 1777 there were no quick ways to move thousands of people. Boatsmen from Canada guided them on the lakes and rivers of upper New York; but when it came to crossing land, the British were very slow. Burgoyne had one message as the force moved toward Ticonderoga: "This Army must not retreat!"

General George Washington, in charge of American forces, was very concerned that Howe was about to attack Philadelphia. He made no effort to reinforce forts in the north, including Ticonderoga. Instead, the troops were kept around the capital for protection. The British attacked Ticonderoga with great coordination. General Philip Schuyler saw no alternative for his American troops stationed there. They were only a small force. He immediately ordered them to retreat. They would give up the fort instead of troops, so that they could fight another day.

After taking Ticonderoga so easily, "Gentleman Johnny" decided to raid some of the nearby farms. He dispatched troops to take cattle and any other supplies from Bennington, Vermont. This would be the beginning of the end of the British. Time and time again, Gentleman Johnny didn't give the American army credit. The small groups of British troops were sitting ducks. American General John Stark made quick work of the British that arrived in Bennington in mid August: 207 British killed, 700 captured.

When Burgoyne heard of this, he was shocked. Normally an optimist, the General started having bad feelings. In late August he had written back to Britain, saying there were fewer Loyalists than they had suspected. "The great bulk of the country," he wrote, "is undoubtedly with the Congress

10

. . . their measures are executed with a secrecy and [efficiency] not to be equalled. Wherever the King's forces point, militia . . . assemble in twenty-four hours. [When] the alarm is over, they return to their farms." But Burgoyne had even more reason to feel ill.

Burgoyne had never actually stated that Howe was to meet him in Albany, New York. But he was counting on it. Word came that Howe was going to attack Philadelphia instead. Supposedly, the British Secretary of State had set aside Howe's orders to be rewritten because he didn't like the handwriting. Through a clerical error, the orders were never sent. Burgoyne's plan was botched — he and his troops were left by themselves in the middle of enemy territory; however, Gentleman Johnny maintained his poise. He wrote back to Britain: "I little foresaw that I was to be left to pursue my way through such a tract of country, and hosts of foes, without any cooperation from New York . . . I yet do not despair." Gentleman Johnny would give it his best shot.

Many Americans felt General Schuyler had given up Ticonderoga too easily, so Congress replaced him as head of the Northern army. His replacement was General Horatio Gates. The American forces gathered outside of Saratoga, New York. They began laying out defensive fortifications, using fallen trees to build walls and digging holes in which to hide. They would be ready when Gentleman Johnny and his redcoats arrived. As the British neared Saratoga, they found the wheat and corn fields ready for picking. The soldiers cut down a lot of these crops to feed their horses. Some residents refused to let this happen. Rather than let the British have her crop, Kitty Schuyler, wife of the General, set all her family's fields afire!

On September 17, Burgoyne got reports that the Americans were moving forward to attack him in great numbers. Only four miles separated them. He saw only one chance, and that was to attack first. Two days later, he did just that. Shortly after 10 A.M., the British cannons roared and 2,000 troops marched forward. Burgoyne had a force of 4,200. But once again he was too relaxed. He had taken his time getting to Saratoga, which had allowed the Americans to build up their own force. Now the American forces were up to 9,000!

Gates had divided the American force into a right and left wing. He commanded the right wing, General Benedict Arnold the left. The Native Americans led the British forces into battle. Many Americans refused to venture into the woods for fear of being scalped by the Indian warriors. The Indians' war whoops struck terror in the Americans.

The British column advanced slowly. Bridges had to be built over gullies and ravines, roads of logs had to be thrown over swamps. The renowned riflemen led by Colonel Daniel Morgan were waiting for the redcoats when they arrived at Freeman's Farm, outside of Saratoga. As the British approached, the Americans opened fire. In their coonskin caps, the Americans blended in with the surroundings — much unlike the red-coated British! Every British officer save one was killed or wounded. The British fell back to the forest. But in moments, the battle changed.

Morgan's men were marksmen, trained to shoot from far-off. As they moved forward in pursuit of the British, they bumped into a wall of redcoats laying in wait. They weren't skilled at hand-to-hand combat. "I am ruined," cried Morgan as his men scattered. British drums rolled, and orders rung out, as the red lines began a slow advance across the field.

But the Americans had their own way of organizing. They practiced some of the first "guerrilla" warfare, a type of battle that relies on using the natural cover of one's surroundings. Morgan had hurried back to the hill to the south of the farm. Here he put a small, cone-shaped horn to his lips and blew. The eerie sound of wild turkey gobbles echoed and reechoed through the woods. All knew what it meant. The familiar "turkey call" rallied his scattered troops. Riflemen and musketmen came pouring out of the woods. From all around, the American troops sprang forward.

The first burst of men crashed into the line of redcoats. But the red line held. The depressed Americans fell back. Suddenly, more American troops came streaming from the south and joined the fray. The fighting was intense. As the American regiments came up, they would fire a volley, then charge across the clearing, only to be hit by British fire. American sharpshooters began picking off the British officers that stood behind the line on horseback. The British were almost broken when a group of 500 German soldiers clamored over the hill. The Americans fell back, and the British survived that day. Most soldiers fell to the ground in exhaustion. The British had lost 600 men. The colonists had lost around 300. Many of the British dead were among their army's top officers.

As was often the case in warfare during this period, neither side pressed for more fighting. If Burgoyne had been able to muster an attack the following day, he would have won easily. But nearly three weeks passed with no action. The armies remained facing each other, while each side helped itself to regroup. Burgoyne wanted to wait for reinforcements that were on their way from the Hudson Valley in New York. But his supplies were running low. On October 5, the British commanders met. They proposed a retreat. Burgoyne was appalled. He countered with a proposal to attack with a portion of their remaining force. Gentleman Johnny was still in charge of his troops. On October 7, the British attacked. But once again, Burgoyne had given the Americans, fighting on their home soil, time to replenish their number of troops. Hearing about the fighting, colonists from all over had dropped their plows for muskets and hurried to Saratoga. The American force had now grown to nearly 16,000.

The British approach was slow, and Burgoyne

finally called for a halt in a wheat field. Their position had a fatal flaw: the flanks, the outermost groups, were very near the forest. The Americans would surely use this cover for an attack. Sure enough, Gates' call went out: "Order out Morgan to begin the battle." The approaching Americans were told to "take the first fire." The British fired, and missed their targets. As was common practice, their officers ordered them to fix the bayonets and charge the rebels. They believed the Americans had also been firing — it was common not to be able to hear enemy fire when in the midst of firing yourself. However, the Americans had held their fire. To the surprise of the British, the Americans fired their own volley and counterattacked. The American fire tore through the approaching British troops.

At the same time, the Americans were able to take over two of the largest British cannons. They turned the great guns on the redcoats. The rest of the Americans burst forward, easily outnumbering the British. Burgoyne, close to the line, could see that the game was up. The British troops began to withdraw. At the same time, a tidal wave of American reinforcements came crashing into the British. The redcoats fled at top speed. If he played his cards correctly, Burgoyne hoped he could flee to Canada without surrendering. At nightfall, Burgoyne began a withdrawal toward Saratoga. The fighting thus far had cost him over 1,000 men.

Commanding his troops to rest in the small village of Saratoga, Burgoyne once again waited too long. The American troops encircled the weakened British. Gates prepared for an attack on October 11. But a British deserter crossed the lines and told Gates that Burgoyne was expecting the attack. Gates wondered if he could trust the deserter, but he chose to hold off the attack. Rather than risk more bloodshed, he would wait out the redcoats.

Completely surrounded, Burgoyne had no choice but to surrender. On October 17, the British surrender was signed. One of the American commanders wrote of the surrender scene:

> General Gates, advised of Burgoyne's approach, met him at the head of his camp, Burgoyne in a rich regal uniform, and Gates in a plain blue frock. When they approached nearly within sword's length, they reined up, and halted. I then named the gentlemen, and General Burgoyne, raising his hat most gracefully, said, "The fortune of war, General Gates, has made me your prisoner," to which the conqueror, returning the courtly salute, promptly replied, "I shall always be ready to bear testimony, that it has not been through any fault of your excellency."

The Americans had won a great victory. But the victory would be worthless if word of it did not reach France. A messenger was sent off immedi-

Surrender of General Burgoyne at Saratoga

ately. It was that same messenger who reached Benjamin Franklin on December 4, 1777. Franklin immediately wrote to the King of France. His message read,

> We have the Honour to acquaint your Excellency that we have just receiv'd an Express from Boston, in 30 days, with the Advice of the total [defeat] of General Burgoyne, himself and his whole Army having surrendered themselves Prisoners.

To the French, the defeat of the British army appeared incredible. It was certainly a signal that

America had a chance to emerge as an independent state. Treaty negotiations began that would bring the French into the war on the American side. First, they would give weapons and supplies. Eventually, they would also contribute troops. Other countries such as Spain also offered their help to the colonists.

By mid-March the treaties were ready to be signed. As was the custom of this age, Franklin had a wig made for this special occasion. However, he found it uncomfortable. Instead, he dressed plainly, without any fancy clothes. The French, who were very extravagant in their dress, had come to admire the casualness of Americans. In Franklin, they saw every American.

As he went forward to sign the treaty, one woman took special note of his dress. "But for his noble face," she later wrote, "I should have taken him for a big farmer, so great was his contrast with the other diplomats, who were all powdered, in full dress, and splashed all over with gold and ribbons."

Through the help of the French, the American "farmers" were able to defeat the British troops. But the French help would have never come had the Battle of Saratoga ended differently. It was this battle that changed the tide of the Revolutionary War.

War with Mexico
THE BATTLE OF BUENA VISTA

During Christmas week of 1846, Americans read about the fate of Lieutenant John Richie. Many U.S. newspapers printed stories such as this one that told his sad tale:

> Lt. Richie was started on his way with important orders from General Winfield Scott, commander of the U.S. military in Mexico, to General Zachary Taylor, whose troops were stationed near the border with Texas. Soldiers traveled with Richie to protect him. But while Richie was getting food for the horses in Monterey, Mexico, a Mexican whirled by on horseback at full speed. With a lasso, the Mexican snatched Richie up and dashed off with his prize at full speed.

* * *

19

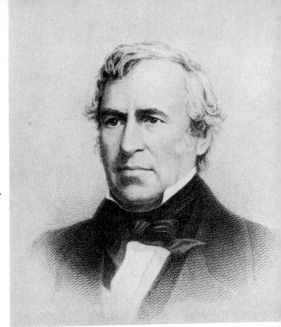

General Zachary Taylor

Richie was found dead the next day; the top secret papers he carried were nowhere to be found. Inside Richie's leather dispatch case the Mexican had found a map and an outline of General Scott's battle plans. He rushed these to Santa Anna, the leader of both Mexico's army and its government. Now the Mexican President-general knew more about the U.S. battle plan than General Taylor.

Reports like this showed Americans that the war with Mexico had gotten very serious. But Americans were still not sure how they felt about this war. This was one reason that up till now the war had been fought only halfheartedly by the United States. For years there had been confusion over who owned the Texas territory, that big chunk of land separating the United States from Mexico. Did it belong to Mexico, the United States, or the Texans themselves? In 1836, Mexico had decided to try and answer this question once and for all. Led by Santa Anna, the Mexicans had invaded Texas and attacked the Texans at the Alamo.

The Texans had been instructed by their leader, Sam Houston, to pull back and not fight the Mexicans at the Alamo. But great fighters such as Jim Bowie and Davy Crockett refused. They felt the Mexicans had to be confronted early. The Texans were beaten badly. The Mexicans had shown no mercy, killing many women and children along with these famous Americans.

Instead of backing down, the Texans used the Alamo to rally their fighting forces. The Texan battle cry became "Remember the Alamo!" And everyone did remember it. The Texans went on to defeat the Mexicans in the Battle of San Jacinto and capture Santa Anna. The Mexican leader recognized Texas as a Republic.

The Texans had made Texas its own nation. However, Mexico had many more people living there. Texans were not sure they could stand up to more Mexican attacks. Texas told the United States it was interested in becoming a state. In 1845 the United States annexed Texas, making it the twenty-eighth state. Any war with Mexico would now include all American forces.

Mexico let the United States know that it considered the annexation of Texas a declaration of war. Fearing trouble, the United States dispatched

President James K. Polk

troops to the border of Texas, its new state. They were led by "Old Rough and Ready," General Zachary Taylor. Taylor had gotten a national reputation for bravery during fights with the Seminole Indians from 1838 to 1840. He wasn't a polished gentleman, but there was no better fighter.

On April 25, 1846, a U.S. scouting party was attacked near the Texas border with Mexico. Taylor sent word to President James K. Polk that there had been "a spilling of American blood on American soil." That was all the President needed to hear. On May 13, 1846, the United States declared war on Mexico. The confusion over who owned Texas would be solved once and for all.

The American public wasn't convinced that the

United States should go to war with Mexico. Was Texas worth it? This war would not be a sure victory, many people said. Even though the United States had a larger population and stronger industry, Mexico had a long and proud military history. In fact, Mexico's army was four times the size of the U.S. Army!

The United States won a few small skirmishes throughout the next month. But President Polk was having trouble deciding how strongly the United States should go after Mexico. Would the American public support a large war? If his troops just kept fighting small battles, the war could drag on and on. He could send more troops, but he wasn't sure he wanted to do that. A major war would present another big problem: Zachary Taylor. Polk had heard that Taylor hoped to be president some day. If he won a war with Mexico, Taylor could, indeed, become the *next* president!

President Polk decided that the war would have to be a major effort. And it wouldn't be under Taylor's control. In addition to sending more troops, Polk sent General Winfield Scott to take over as commander of the U.S. army that was to invade central Mexico. Scott was a trustworthy veteran of many wars. He was not as unpredictable and headstrong as Taylor. Scott would also take new battle plans with him. He would lead the troops against mainland Mexico and its capital, Mexico City. To do so, he took thousands of Taylor's best troops. Taylor and his depleted forces were left alone in northern Mexico, near the Texas border.

The information that Santa Anna intercepted from Lieutenant Richie told him all these secrets. The Mexican leader had to choose whether he should defend his capital city against Scott's large attack — so great an attack that he may not have been able to defeat it — or lead his troops north after Taylor and his weakened army. Santa Anna had about 24,500 men; Taylor was down to only 4,000. Santa Anna chose to go north. He would surprise Taylor, and find out if he really was "Old Rough and Ready."

It was February of 1847. When Mexican countrymen told Taylor that Santa Anna was marching north, Taylor replied with disbelief. "Bosh," he said. "How can an army get through that country, especially at this time of year? How many horses, wagons, and pack mules would it take just to haul the food?" The troops serving under the general liked the way Taylor was less jumpy than some of the other commanders. Other commanders had put them on alert at the slightest rumor. They trusted Taylor's judgment.

Suddenly, Taylor's scouts rode in with the news. It was true! "Santa Anna's marching hard at us," they told him. "His cavalry (troops on horseback) gobbled up some of our patrols." Now the general had something to worry about. Several miles up the road, was a ranch named Buena Vista. At this ranch, there was a pass in the road filled with deep gulches, gullies, and a stream with steep banks carving up the land. The commanders decided they'd wait there for the enemy.

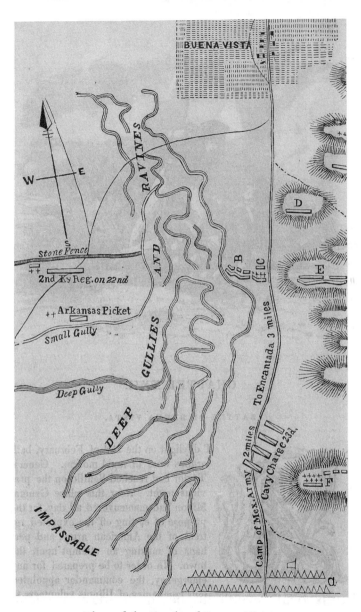

Plan of the Battle of Buena Vista

25

A handful of Texas's best troops, the Texas Rangers, galloped into Taylor's camp the next day. They had scouted the Mexicans. "Comin' straight at us," they reported. "They have way over ten thousand. Outnumber us three to one." Taylor pulled the remaining troops back to the Buena Vista pass. It looked like the battle was really going to happen.

When Santa Anna heard the enemy was moving backward, he was furious. "Taylor's in full retreat!" he thought. "I've come all this way and now they want to retreat!" He took all his troops on horseback and galloped ahead. He would not let the gringos get away! They found the Americans near Buena Vista. Santa Anna sent a letter on to Taylor. It read,

> You are surrounded by 20,000 men. [You will] be cut to pieces. But as you deserve from me consideration and particular esteem, I wish to save you from a catastrophe. . . . To this end you will be granted one hour's time to surrender.

This wasn't the way you treated a warrior such as Taylor. He boomed with laughter when he read the note. Old Rough and Ready surrender? That would be the day! He immediately sent off his message to the Mexican leader, declining this offer.

The two armies were so close that they could see one another. In the morning, as the American drums beat reveille to begin the day, Mexican priests could be seen saying Mass to their troops.

Mexican army officers

A panicked scout rode down from the hills and reported to Taylor. "About a thousand Mexican cavalrymen are up there in the hills riding around us," he said. "They are getting in our rear to cut us off." The Mexicans were trying to surround them! Taylor immediately rode to the rear to check out the situation.

General Taylor had thought his army was in a strong position in the mountain pass. Now he realized it was weak because it stretched only three thousand yards across. It could be outflanked from behind. And that was what the Mexicans were doing at that very moment. The U.S. artillery dashed forward with horse-drawn cannons. They fired long and hard at the Mexicans trying to sneak in from behind. Finally, the Mexican division fell back, defeated. But none of the other Mexicans knew they had not been able to surround the Americans. They believed their attack was going as planned.

Santa Anna ordered another division to attack from the front. The soldiers responded, fearlessly riding into the gully. The American forces were ready; there were no Mexicans in the rear to divert their attention. The Mexicans were slaughtered by the awaiting Americans. The Mexicans had many more soldiers than the Americans. An all-out attack would have overwhelmed the depleted U.S. forces. But Santa Anna chose to use many attacks, each with only small numbers of troops. His piecemeal attacks were helping the outnumbered U.S. troops.

Scouts finally pointed out the American weakness to the Mexican leader. Not only was the enemy front line very short, but to the east, near the mountains, the ravines were not deep, and it would be easy to scramble down and out of them. This was where his troops would attack the gringos. Santa Anna led his foot soldiers straight at the Americans' left flank.

One American commander saw the Mexicans coming and ordered his troops to withdraw. Confusion took over. Other American troops saw their retreating comrades, and assumed they should do the same. General Taylor arrived from the rear just

28

in the nick of time. A battlefield panic is a hard thing to stop. But Taylor was the man for the job. With the aid of the troops that arrived with him, the fleeing troops were stopped. They turned and resumed battle.

Just as Santa Anna ordered his last division into attack, a cannonball came flying at him. It knocked him to the ground and killed his horse. Santa Anna was a proud man who had lost part of one leg in battle earlier in his life. The fall had hurt his amputated leg, but he would not show it. Dazed and hurt, the Mexican general mounted an aid's horse and continued onward. He pointed his long sword at the mountain range to the east. That was where it would all happen. The Mexicans came strong. They overwhelmed the first level of U.S. guns. It was fierce fighting, but the Mexicans' great number of troops was too much for the Americans. Slowly, the Mexicans rose up the hills on the east side of the Buena Vista pass.

The U.S. forces on the west side of the ravine saw what was taking place to the east. They had to figure out a way to help their comrades or the battle would soon be over. They galloped across the road straight at the Mexicans. It looked like they weren't going to stop, as if they would charge right into the Mexican troops. But at the last minute, the U.S. forces stopped and wheeled around. Taylor yelled, "Double-shot your guns and give 'em hell!" And that's just what they did, firing their cannons and guns into the Mexican troops climbing up the hillside. Now the Mexicans were sur-

Battle of Buena Vista

rounded, and under heavy fire from every direction.

The Mexicans suddenly wheeled and ran south in surrender. In an instant, the battle had swung from the Mexicans' advantage. Now the American troops celebrated their hard-fought victory. The Americans had lost 740 men. Santa Anna's faulty leadership had cost his country between 1,550 and 2,000 soldiers. Most of his beaten men no longer believed in him as their leader. Their will to fight had been broken.

The Americans shared their supplies and water with the wounded Mexicans and gave them first aid. It was a long road back home for the Mexicans. The journey was made longer by the knowledge that they had lost a battle they should have won. Mexico would never recover from its defeat at Buena Vista.

Taylor's victory at Buena Vista showed the Americans that they could beat the Mexicans, and that is was a fight worth fighting. General Scott's assaults on Mexico City and other important Mexican sites would put an end to the war. It would be over by 1848. For his victory at Buena Vista, Taylor became a national hero. In 1848, Zachary Taylor, war hero, proved President Polk correct — he was elected the twelfth president of the United States.

Rallied behind the war against Mexico by Taylor's heroics, Americans finally believed that this was an important war. They made up a song to show their support for the troops. It immortalized Taylor, his troops, and that fearful day in February of 1847, at the Buena Vista pass.

BUENA VISTA

Near Buena Vista's mountain chain,
Hurrah! Hurrah! Hurrah!
Brave Taylor met his foes again,
Hurrah! Hurrah! Hurrah!
Though thousands to our tens appear,
Our boys have hearts that know no fear,
Hurrah! Hurrah! Hurrah!
Hurrah! Hurrah! Hurrah!

That day heard Santa Anna boast,
Hurrah! Hurrah! Hurrah!

Ere night he'd vanquish all our host,
Hurrah! Hurrah! Hurrah!
But then the braggard did not know
That Taylor never yields to foe!
Hurrah! Hurrah! Hurrah!

No page in history e'er can show
Hurrah! Hurrah! Hurrah!
So bright a victory o'er a foe
Hurrah! Hurrah! Hurrah!
As we this day did proudly gain
On Buena Vista's bloody plain!
Hurrah! Hurrah! Hurrah!

The American Civil War
THE FIRST BATTLE OF BULL RUN

The roads outside of Centreville, Virginia, looked little like a battlefield on this fine July morning. From Manassas Junction to Bull Run, it looked like some sort of park. The hills were filled with people in their best dress. Many were reporters, ready to cover the first battle of the war between the North and the South. Many others were congressmen and their families, or just residents of the area who had come to view the battle. Most now sat safely atop hills, their picnic breakfasts and lunches spread around them.

The conflict between the northern and southern United States had been played out in Congress and in newspapers for years. There were many differences between the southern and northern portions of the United States. But the greatest was their ways of making money. The northeast had many large factories. Thousands of European immigrants worked in these factories for low wages.

The south, on the other hand, depended on large farms to grow crops such as cotton and tobacco. These farms were worked by slaves, usually African-Americans. They were usually traded and sold, and rarely paid for their labor. Their "owners" often treated them cruelly. For decades, arguments had raged over the issue of slavery.

Northerners decided it was cruel and immoral for people to keep slaves. But Southerners refused to get rid of their slaves. For years, the country moved forward with this major difference in philosophies. When new lands west of the Mississippi River opened, Southerners demanded that slavery be allowed there, too. Many Northerners didn't want to have slavery extend to more states. This stalemate continued until 1860, when Abraham Lincoln was elected the sixteenth president of the United States. Everyone knew that Lincoln was a Northerner from Illinois. He had once stated, "A house divided against itself cannot stand. I believe this government cannot endure permanently half slave and half free."

Fearing that Lincoln's election would be harmful to Southern interests, South Carolina seceded from the United States. Florida, Georgia, Alabama, Mississippi, Louisiana, and Texas soon followed. Together these states formed the Confederate States of America. At his inauguration later that year, Lincoln warned the Southerners that they had control over whether or not a Civil War would be fought — he would not order an attack against them. Confederate cannons fired on

Union Fort Sumter, South Carolina, in April, 1861. With war at hand, four more states joined the Confederacy.

The Confederacy had been able to enjoy their victory at Fort Sumter for only a short time. Every state in the Union had whipped together troops immediately. Only the Potomac River separated the Confederacy from Washington, DC, and the North. By early July, Washington, DC, was filled with Union soldiers to protect it from invasion. Now, on July 16, 1861, the first meeting of the South's Congress was only days away. Such a meeting would be the first illustration of the South's separateness from the Union. Everyone knew a country could not be run by two governments.

A battle would have to be fought. And everyone in Washington, DC, knew it would be a short fight. The Union Army was the well-drilled and well-supplied American army, while the South had thrown together a ragged force only in the last few months. Most likely, there would not even be any fighting — the Rebels would see the force they were up against and surrender. Most people expected this to be the beginning of the end for the rebellious southern spirit. Many of the picnickers on this day had decided they should see the battle while it lasted.

Near Centreville, one could see occasional groups of Union soldiers marching back toward Washington. These were some of the men who had volunteered for three months service after April

General Irvin McDowell

15, 1861, following the Southern attack on Fort Sumter.

At that time, there had been a great war scare. But now these men's time was up and they were going home. The largest Union force in the area was under the command of General Irvin McDowell. In the next few days, the term of service would expire for most of his remaining 30,000 troops. Most people agreed that the battle would have to take place before these soldiers left.

McDowell felt his troops were not ready for battle, but he had to fight while he still had an army. Early on the morning of July 21, 1861, he ordered an attack on Confederate troops near Manassas.

Pierre Beauregard

These 20,000 rebel troops were defending the main railroad line in Manassas which led to important regions of Virginia. Commanded by Pierre Beauregard, the Confederates held a line along Bull Run, a small stream between Manassas Junction and Centreville.

McDowell and Beauregard had attended military college at West Point together in 1838. Like many of the soldiers in the Civil War, these enemy officers had been comrades only months prior. For some families, sons and fathers fought on opposing sides of the war. Both armies contained recruits from North and South, depending on which side enlistees had favored in the war.

Another small Southern army, about 12,000 strong, was located to the south and commanded by General Joseph Johnston. McDowell was counting on Union general Robert Patterson to keep Johnston's men busy while the fighting went on to the north. However, Johnston learned of McDowell's attack plan and moved his entire army to Manassas to join Beauregard. Johnston's men were able to move quickly by using the railroad. It was the first time an American army had moved to battle by train. This gave armies a quick way to move soldiers to battle sites. Late in the war, the North's better railways would help them greatly in the moving and supplying of their troops.

Most of Johnston's troops had arrived by July 21. When the Union attack took place, the rebel forces were much stronger than expected. Colonel Nathan "Shanks" Evans was commanding the 1,100 Confederates who defended the only bridge over Bull Run. As Evans watched the Union forces attack, he ordered a counterattack of his own. Led by Major Roberdeau Wheat, a huge, 275-pound man, the group from Louisiana ran forward, waving their bowie knives (long-bladed knives named after frontiersman James Bowie). They were able to tie up the Union troops momentarily, but they could not hold for long.

The first Union attack was driven back. But a full attack followed that pummelled the left flank of the Confederate line. McDowell sent off a messenger to President Abraham Lincoln telling him that they were winning the battle. *The New York*

Battle of Bull Run

Times wanted to break the story first and quickly came out with an exciting account of the "victory." The headline read, "CRUSHING REBELLION: The Greatest Battle Ever Fought on this Continent, Fearful Carnage on Both Sides — THE REBELS ROUTED."

The Confederate troops met up at Henry House Hill and set up a new line to stop the Union troops. In the center of this Confederate line was a brigade led by General Thomas Jackson. The troops on every side of Jackson's began to flee upon seeing the approaching Union forces. Suddenly, one of their commanders saw Jackson's troops standing firm in the center. At this impressive sight he turned to his men and shouted, "There stands

*General Thomas
"Stonewall" Jackson*

Jackson like a stone wall! Rally behind [them]!"
This moment turned the tide of this battle, and
gave Jackson the nickname he would carry for the
rest of his life — Stonewall.

The Union troops pressed on, but Jackson's brigade stayed firm as the stone wall to which they
had been compared. For more than three hours
the fight raged for the Henry House Hill. The in-
experienced soldiers on both sides fought bravely,
but by mid-afternoon it looked as though the
Northerners would win.

Suddenly, a group of men stepped from the
woods in front of the Union line. At this time,
soldiers from both the North and South were uni-

formed in many different ways. Most Union troops wore blue, but many wore whatever clothing they had. The soldiers before the Union line were Confederates from Virginia. But they happened to be wearing blue uniforms. In the confusion, the Union line held its fire. The Virginians walked to within seventy yards of the Union troops and then opened fire. Said one officer who was observing from a far-off hill, "It seemed as though every man and horse of that battery just laid right down and died."

At about this same time, Johnston's last brigade arrived at Manassas Junction. They were a group of Texans commanded by General Kirby-Smith. "Take them to the front," growled Johnston. "Go where the fire is hottest." They ran straight from the station and into the Union line. These fresh troops were too much for McDowell's tired Union soldiers. The whole line panicked. In a few moments all the Union troops were in flight back across Bull Run. A Confederate officer later wrote, "The whole field was a confused swarm of men, like bees, running away as fast as their legs could carry them." To add to the confusion, the terrified picnickers were now trying desperately to return to Washington.

A dejected General McDowell sent off a dispatch to Lincoln:

> The victory seemed complete. But our men, exhausted with fatigue and thirst

and confused by firing into each other, were attacked by the enemy reserves and driven back. . . .

The men have thrown away their haversacks in the battle and are without food. They have eaten nothing since breakfast. We are out of artillery ammunition. The larger part of the men are a confused mob, entirely demoralized.

The next day *The New York Times* headline read: "DISASTER TO THE NATIONAL ARMY: Retreat of McDowell's Command, 90,000 Rebels in the Field: A PANIC AMONG TEAMSTERS AND CIVILIANS." The defeat at Bull Run showed the North that the Union could be preserved only by a long and costly war. Confederate leaders realized that they needed better-trained men, but that this was a war that they could win.

In the North, the public was stunned. The picnickers had glimpsed firsthand the violence that this war would involve. The Civil War would claim more American lives than all other American wars combined. You have to remember, in this war *both* sides were Americans. In this battle alone, 2,708 Union troops and 1,982 Confederates had been killed. This adds up to nearly 5,000 dead Americans! A nation torn apart, brother fighting brother, the First Battle of Bull Run had been a rude awakening to everyone — North or South — living in the United States.

This First Battle of Bull Run left a lasting

impression on its participants and viewers. One Union officer explained: "We're all coming out of Virginny as far as we can and pretty well whipped, too. . . . I'm going home. I've had enough of fighting to last my lifetime." All the returning soldiers shared the sentiments of another Union soldier, who said: "I can truly say that I have seen all the horrors of war." But the truth was that there was much more to come.

The American Civil War
THE BATTLE OF GETTYSBURG

The soldiers were not the only ones troubled at the way the war had progressed. In the streets of the North, many civilians began questioning the war with the South. Since the beginning of the war, there had been a group of Northerners who did not approve of the war. They were called "copperheads." During the winter of 1862–63, with no end to the war in sight, and with more and more young men being killed in battle or drafted off to war, the number of copperheads grew steadily.

When it had begun, many Americans believed this would be a quick war, without much bloodshed. Now, thousands of lives had been lost. Normal life was impossible throughout the United States. Battles had destroyed many of the homes, businesses, and farms that Americans had worked hard to build. More and more Americans wondered whether or not all this sacrifice was worthwhile. Many of these Northerners decided the war

*Confederacy President
Jefferson Davis*

was not worth it and they also became copperheads. That winter was the lowest point for Union morale.

Confederacy President Jefferson Davis and General Robert E. Lee had spies living in the North that kept them abreast of these changes. If they could give the North one more taste of the war — on their own soil — maybe the public opinion could be swayed by the copperheads. Maybe the legislators could then be pressured to end the war.

The call went out: The Confederates would invade the North.

This, however, was not a typical invasion. As the Confederates crossed the Potomac River into

Maryland, General Lee issued orders that his men were not to destroy any of the towns they passed through. In essence, the Confederates were trying to flush out the Union army — nothing more. Unfortunately, they had to do so without their "eyes and ears." Before the days of radar and satellite pictures, armies depended on their cavalry to keep them posted on the enemy's position. The troops on horseback would ride far out ahead of the foot soldiers and scout out the enemy, often following them. They would send messages back that field generals would use to design battle plans.

The Confederacy's crackerjack cavalry was commanded by General Jeb Stuart. Stuart loved daring challenges. On the march north, Stuart had gotten a report of a Union wagon train of supplies passing nearby. He had set off with his troops to hijack the supplies for the Confederacy. Now, Lee's troops had to move north without cavalry — and Lee was not happy about it. His army was making this march "deaf and blind." Marching with Lee was his great friend General James Longstreet, "Old Pete." Stonewall Jackson, one of the Confederacy's greatest leaders, had been lost just months earlier at Chancellorsville.

The leadership of the Confederacy had been solid throughout the war. It was one of the army's greatest strengths. However, this was partly because the Confederates were the underdogs — little was expected of their army. The Union, on the other hand, was supposed to easily defeat its enemy. Only the leadership could be blamed for its inability to do this. For this reason, another failed invasion attempt by General Hooker moved Lincoln to replace his head of the Union army once again. General George Meade was given command of the remaining army. The mission Lincoln gave him was simple, but overwhelming: defeat Lee's army; conquering cities alone would not win the war — the army must be crushed.

With over 60,000 troops in all, the Confederates crossed into the North in three groups. General Richard Ewell marched first. After spending the last months in war-ravaged Virginia, the troops marched into another world: huge barns full of goods, cozy towns, and fields of ripening wheat filled the valleys.

General George Meade

All along their march, the Confederates were in full view of the Northern citizens. With the noise and time needed to move troops, Civil War battles were rarely a surprise. Confederate soldiers stopped in Northern towns to buy food and other goods. The call flew up the coast that Lee had invaded the North. It was only a matter of where the Union troops would gather to meet him. General Meade, the man making this decision, had been in command only one day when he received the news!

That Sunday night, a weary spy came to Lee bearing staggering news. The whole Federal Army had crossed the Potomac and was marching north. They were coming up fast behind the Confederates. Lee knew what it meant: his invasion had to be stopped. The troops must gather and set themselves in open country. They must prepare for battle. In each previous battle, only portions of each army had clashed. Never before had so many Confederate and Union troops been this close to one another. The total number of soldiers was 163,000. This was shaping up to be one of the war's most important battles. Lee looked over maps, and sent a message for Ewell to meet him near Gettysburg, a small farming town in Pennsylvania.

The entire region was braced for war. Northern news correspondents set out to catch up with the Union army. Washington, DC, was described as a "city beseiged. . . . All night long, troops . . . marching; orderlies with clanking sabres. . . ." The streets of Baltimore, Maryland were barricaded with tar barrels to prevent Confederate troops passage. The Union Headquarters was set up near Gettysburg in Taneytown, Pennsylvania. The first order of business was to locate the enemy. Scouting troops traveled all over the countryside to find the Confederates. Their search would have been simple if they had known one important fact: many of the Confederate troops were in need of shoes.

The only shoe factory in the area was in Gettysburg. Many of the Confederate soldiers traveled into town and to the factory. Once the Confederates had been spotted buying their shoes, the Union troops were called together to converge on Gettysburg. By chance alone, this quiet Pennsylvania town was set to become the site of the nation's most historic battle.

When Lee realized this was to be the site of battle, he ordered the troops to take control of the town and a long, narrow hill to the west, Seminary Ridge. On the other side of town, Union troops immediately seized what they viewed as the most important sites: Cemetery Hill and Culp's Hill. These were critical because they were the highest points in the area. From there, they could look down over the entire battlefield. And, if they could get them up the hills, cannons could be fired without danger from Confederates. Early on July 1, the Union began setting up battle stations. Skirmishes flared throughout Gettysburg. These skirmishes were brief, but quite costly: one of them claimed the life of John F. Reynolds, one of the Union's best generals.

On Cashtown Road, a main thoroughfare leading to Gettysburg, the fighting turned into all-out battle. No one had authorized the battle, and a concerned Lee watched as a full-fledged battle grew out of the skirmishes. Suddenly, rows of Confederate troops who were returning from an earlier excursion marched in behind the Federal line by chance. The Union soldiers turned to flee. Lee saw this as an opportunity for a total victory. He gave the order to attack. As the gray-coated Confederates moved in, the Union blue coats streamed through the town, running for the safety of their camps. Finally, the fighting stopped for the evening. That night, a concerned General Meade could be heard murmuring: "Tomorrow, gentlemen, we fight the decisive battle of the war." But when would Lee's attack come? No one could be sure.

General Lee wanted to attack early on July 2, 1863. However, General James Longstreet was interested in fighting a defensive battle. "Old Pete" Longstreet was one of Lee's most trusted advisers — but their difference of opinion wasn't what prevented Lee's attack in the early morning. Longstreet also commanded over one third of the Confederate forces. He claimed his army was simply not ready to fight an offensive campaign. In his calm way, Lee convinced Old Pete of what had to be done. Still, Longstreet's men wouldn't be ready to lead the attack until early afternoon.

On the Union side, General Dan Sickel decided to change General Meade's battle plan. He led his men off Cemetery Ridge toward the Confederate line. As the troops neared the peach orchard that separated them from the Confederates, 160 cannons opened up on them. Across the valley was the eerie Devil's Den, a huge rock formation with deep crevices wide enough for a person to slide into. Confederate sharpshooters had hidden in these cracks, making themselves nearly impossible to hit. They joined in on the attack on Sickel's men. The general had unknowingly led his men into a trap. Over 250 additional Union troops were ordered to make a bayonet charge to save what remained of Sickel's regiment. The trapped soldiers were freed, but 215 of these additional men were lost in the process.

On the Confederate side, Longstreet was still dragging his feet. He was trying to delay the attack until Stuart's cavalry returned and until General George Pickett's troops had arrived. "General Lee is a little nervous," Old Pete said in conversation. "He wants me to attack, but I don't wish to do so without General Pickett. I never go into battle with one boot off."

For this reason, the Confederate attacks began only piecemeal, one at a time. They crossed Devil's Den and confronted the Union line in small groups. Devil's Den was separated from Cemetery Ridge (the Union position) by a broad valley filled with smooth, round rocks. There was no forest or any place to hide. By attacking in small groups, the Confederates suffered heavy casualties.

Meanwhile, Meade ordered his engineers to scout the rest of the surrounding land. They found two high areas still free. Troops were immediately sent to secure Round Top and Little Round Top, two hills that would allow control of the entire valley. The Union forces raised their cannons to these high points with incredible difficulty. They were each hauled by rope up and over the rocks!

But the Confederates were also moving toward these positions, and Longstreet's men had already begun to climb the hills. From these points, the Confederates would dominate the entire Union position. As the Confederates continued their climb, they were met by heavy Union fire from the top of the plateaus. One Union commander on the top of Round Top wrote, "All was astir now on our crest . . . the men were all in their places, and you might have heard the rattle of 10,000 ramrods as they 'thugged' upon the little globes and cones of lead." (Civil War soldiers were slowed by their muskets, which had to be reloaded after each shot.) But the Union troops had arrived on these hills just in time. They were led by General G. K. Warren. By keeping Longstreet and the Confederates from these hills, Warren is given credit for saving the Battle of Gettysburg for the Union.

The major Confederate attack began on July 3, 1863. By early morning, Pickett's troops had arrived, as had Stuart's cavalry. Everything was in order. Two hours of Confederate cannon fire rained down on Union positions. Correspondent Samuel Wilkeson described the scene: "As many as 6 [cannon shots] in a second . . . bursting and screaming in the yard . . . hitched horses reared

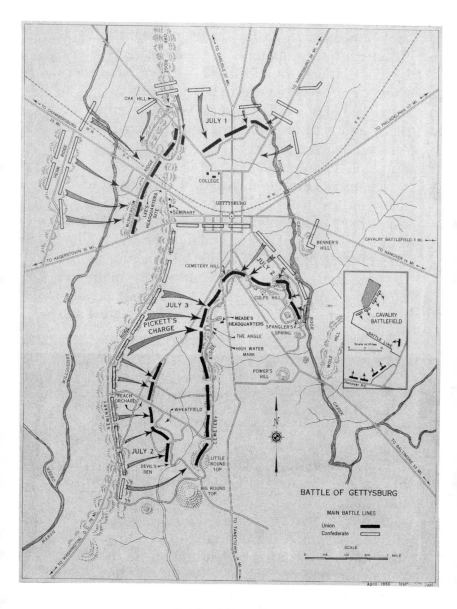

Battle of Gettysburg

53

and plunged . . . 16 lay dead and mangled, still fastened to their halters." A great shrieking could be heard. It was the rebel yell — the call that every Confederate whooped as they began to charge. The rebel yell sent chills through veteran Union soldiers, and made many young soldiers turn and flee. All who heard it knew that, through the thick cannon smoke, an attack was on its way.

"Up, men!" Pickett shrieked. "Don't forget today that you are from old Virginia! Good-bye, boys, Good-bye!" Suddenly, massive groups of Confederates swept out of hiding and into the open valley. The famous Pickett's Charge had begun, as the dashing general led 15,000 troops — many no more than nineteen years old — across the valley that separated the armies. It was the greatest single attack of the Civil War.

Union cannons, numbering almost two hundred, opened fire from Little Round Top. They blasted huge holes in the approaching line. Horses fell and the screams of injured soldiers drowned out the rebel yell. Smoke filled the air. Thousands of men grappled at close quarters. Suddenly, the Union troops swept down from their secure hiding places and toward the Confederates. This proved too much for them, and Pickett and his remaining men turned back.

Lee had watched the attack first with admiration, then with horror. Sending so many of his troops on one charge, across such a large open area had been the worst mistake of his military career — no matter how bravely Pickett had car-

General Robert E. Lee

ried out the charge. Some wounded men crawled back to safety; others needed to use their muskets as crutches. Lee skillfully withdrew his troops and immediately retreated over the Potomac River and back to Virginia. Over seventeen miles of Confederate wagons, full of wounded, made the trip. Meade could have pursued, but he was just thankful for the Union's first clear-cut victory in the eastern battles.

In the late afternoon of July 4, a Union band appeared on Cemetery Ridge, overlooking the incredible scene. They played "Yankee Doodle," "Hail to the Chief," and "The Star Spangled Banner." But below them, thousands lying in the fields would never hear these songs. The dead were literally heaped and strewn throughout the valley. There were hundreds of dead horses, as well. It would be weeks before the people of Gettysburg could draw a breath without getting a sickening reminder of what had taken place there. The Union had lost 23,000 men; the Confederates, 28,000. One quarter of the Confederate casualties had come during Pickett's Charge.

It would take two more long years of fighting and many more great battles to catch General Lee's army. After the battle of Appomattox, Lee knew his side had been beaten. On April 9, 1865,

Ulysses S. Grant

Lee waited for the head of the Union army, Ulysses S. Grant, to arrive before surrendering. As a gesture of respect, Grant allowed Confederate officers to keep their swords, and their horses. He then gave General Lee food for 25,000 men. Lee rose and walked out of the farmhouse without a word. For the most part, the American Civil War was over.

The tide of the entire war had changed in the small Pennsylvania town, chosen purely by chance. There were other historic battles in the Civil War, but Gettysburg is the site that history remembers most. On November 19, 1863, the National Cemetery was dedicated in Gettysburg, on top of Cemetery Ridge. At this time, oratory (or public speaking) was a respected skill and a popular way of spending time. The star of this day was the Massachusetts minister, Edward Everett. He was known as the greatest orator in the United States. People turned out in droves to hear this famous speaker. They listened patiently while he spoke for three hours!

As part of the ceremony, President Abraham Lincoln was scheduled to perform the actual dedication. After the great speaker had received a rousing hand for his long-winded speech, Lincoln stepped to the podium and spoke only a hundred words. What he said was very simple, and it did not take him more than two or three minutes. But those words are now among the most famous in our nation's history.

President Abraham Lincoln delivering the Gettysburg Address

We all know these words for what they mean to us about America. As you read them on the next page, try to imagine what they meant to Americans in 1863. Battles such as Gettysburg had left Americans wondering how this war could be worth all of this terror. How could anything be worth that?

In a few short sentences, Abraham Lincoln told them why it was worth it. His words retell us today why the sacrifices of battle continue to be worthwhile. The people who left Cemetery Ridge that day knew that some things were indeed worth fighting for.

* * *

The Gettysburg Address

Fourscore and seven years ago our fathers brought forth upon this continent a new nation . . . dedicated to the idea that all men are created equal. Now we are in a great civil war. We are here on a great battlefield of that war. We have come to dedicate a portion of this field as a final resting-place for those who here gave their lives that this nation might live.

We here highly resolve that these dead shall not have died in vain; that this nation, under God, shall have a new birth of freedom, and that the Government of the people, by the people, and for the people shall not perish from the earth.

War with Spain
THE BATTLE OF SAN JUAN HILL

With a squeak, the chair shifted backward with the man's weight. The middle-sized man leaned back and stared at the ceiling. He wondered who he could trust. He needed answers, but it seemed as if there was no one to ask. Where could he find the *truth*? This could have been any businessman, a father, or a wealthy investor. Someone too insignificant to have access to the proper lines of information. But, actually, this was none other than U.S. President William McKinley.

On his desk in front of him lay today's newspaper. The headline on it read: "300 CUBAN WOMEN BUTCHERED!" Headlines such as this had been appearing throughout 1897. Usually, they were based on lies or half-truths. But could one be sure these terrible things weren't really happening? President McKinley couldn't be sure, and it was driving him crazy! The American public was even less calm. Many Americans were fed up with

President William McKinley

what they read about Cuba. They were calling for war.

Such a war would be fought against Spain, the country that controlled Cuba. American newspapers had reported that it was the Spanish who were doing terrible things to the Cubans. The Cuban people were starving while Spanish landowners lived in luxury. For years, Cuban rebels and the Spanish army had been fighting a bloody war. The Spanish had rounded up thousands of Cubans and thrown them into prison camps. People were starved and tortured. The American public wanted a war that would free the Cubans from the cruel Spanish rule.

61

But there was more to this story than met the eye — that is why McKinley couldn't be sure of his course of action. Two important New York newspapers were locked in a circulation war, each trying to sell more papers than the other. The Spanish-American conflict had become their tool for winning this newspaper battle. The publishers of each newspaper found that sensational stories about Cuba served two purposes: The coverage aroused support for the Cuban rebels and, more importantly, it sold papers.

When there were no stories to print, reporters were told to make them up. One of these papers, the New York *Morning Journal*, was run by the wealthy William Randolph Hearst, one of the most famous newspapermen of all time. He sent a well-known artist, Frederic Remington, to Cuba to sketch the fighting between the Cubans and Spanish. When Remington telegraphed back that he wanted to quit because all was calm in Havana, Hearst reportedly replied: "You furnish the pictures and I'll furnish the war." Hearst and other newspapermen had decided they could make up the news, or at least make it more interesting. This was one of the first examples of the press influencing the opinions of its readers. Creating stories that were made up in order to shock or thrill readers became known as *yellow journalism*.

President McKinley opposed war with Spain. He had served in the Civil War only thirty years prior. His firsthand view of war had scared him for life. He felt he could never support another one. And he definitely believed the United States had not yet fully recovered from the Civil War. But many Americans felt otherwise.

After the Civil War, many Americans had moved west and settled in new portions of the country. This expansion had been foremost in the lives of most Americans. But as the century came to a close, many Americans were looking for new challenges for their nation. The United States had all the wealth and natural resources it could want. And many people believed it was time for the United States to use its wealth to begin moving into new parts of the world. With such great advantages, the United States could influence many countries and become a power in international trade. Many people felt that the first step of this plan should be war with Spain. Such a war would make the United States look good for helping a neighbor, Cuba, as well as open up new trade opportunities.

The debate continued into 1898, when there came reports of riots in the streets of Havana and other Cuban cities. The United States was concerned for the safety of Americans in Cuba. The pressure on McKinley grew more intense. In response, President McKinley ordered a fleet of war ships to Havana. They were on a friendly visit to protect Americans working in Havana. Only one ship, the *Maine*, was anchored directly in Havana Harbor. However, there were other U.S. ships patrolling areas further from shore. On the surface, the Cubans and Spanish gave the captain and crew of the *Maine* a warm reception. However, many

Spanish resented the Yankee ship's presence.

On February 15, Captain Charles Sigsbee completed his regular inspection of the *Maine*. All was in order, so he retired to his cabin. No sooner had he reached his quarters than a huge explosion burst through his ship. Fire spread throughout the ship, making its way toward the ammunition. Massive explosions tore the ship open. Smoke and flames trapped many crew members below deck. In moments, the ship sank, killing 260 American crew members.

No one knew what had caused the initial explosion. But that didn't stop the two New York newspapers from telling their own story. "MAINE EXPLOSION CAUSED BY BOMB OR TORPEDO?" read the headline in one paper. To these papers, there was no doubt the explosion had been a deliberate Spanish attack — the only question was what had caused it. Americans read this and felt there was no doubt that Spain had attacked a U.S. ship — and that meant it was time for war. Men and women wore buttons on their coats that read, "Remember the *Maine*."

The Spanish insisted that an accident on board the ship had caused the disaster. McKinley refused to declare war; instead, he chose to wait for the official Navy report on the incident. He knew that the U.S. Army of 28,000 was ill prepared for war. But this excuse was satisfying fewer Americans every day. The public began to criticize McKinley more than ever.

When the Navy report finally arrived, it did little

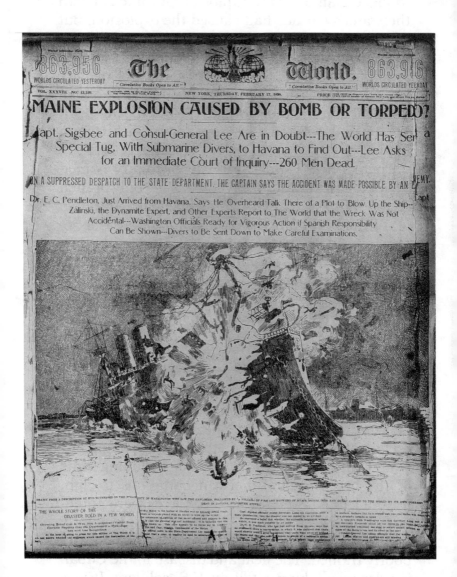

The explosion of the Maine

to place blame for the explosion. A mine beneath the water's surface had caused the explosion, but no one could tell who had placed it there. Despite this news, McKinley could not stand the pressure any longer. He feared that if he did not declare war he would lose control of the Republican political party, and not be reelected. On April 11, 1898, he asked Congress to declare war on Spain.

Thanks to a young Assistant Secretary named Theodore Roosevelt, the Navy was the only branch of the military ready to confront Spain. It did so off of the Philippine Islands. Commodore George Dewey easily defeated the Spanish in Manila Bay, but then he had to sit and wait. He didn't have any force with which to invade on land, and the United States had none prepared. Such a force was on its way, however. Over one million men — many, veterans of the Civil War — had volunteered for service. Soon the fighting continued in other areas, including Cuba.

The war planners had tried to take into consideration Cuba's tropical climate and terrain when devising their battle plan. Special cavalry divisions on horseback would do much of the fighting. They would be followed by foot soldiers, including some of the first African-American battalions to fight for the United States. The U.S. forces were potentially much greater than those of Spain. But early in the war, U.S. forces were uncoordinated and poorly trained. The heat and disease in the Cuban jungles was taking a toll on U.S. soldiers. It was not until late June that these troops were able to gather and make a strong push toward the important Spanish stronghold in Santiago.

Up till now the war had been only frustrating for the Americans. They had been breaking their way through the jungle for weeks. However, this was the Spanish soldiers' home territory. They knew this island very well. Just as the Americans had been able to defeat the British in the Revolutionary War by using guerrilla tactics, the Spanish were much more suited to fighting here in the jungle. The bugs and heat had left many Americans too ill to fight — even one of the commanders had to remain in his tent for much of the fighting. The leaders of the long column of men on the jungle trail especially had problems. The jungle was too thick to walk through unless you stuck to the trails. But the trails were only wide enough for one soldier to pass. The Spanish were hiding in trenches on the hills all around the trails. They simply had to watch the trail's mouth and shoot. When the Americans appeared, the Spanish would aim and fire. And the Americans had no choice but to continue on the trail.

Two hills lay directly ahead of the American position. Each had Spanish artillery atop it. First, the Americans fired to see what the Spanish had. The Spanish answer was dreadful: shrapnel shells exploded above the trees and sent steel balls and tiny scraps of metal raining down on the American line. The American cannons tried to answer, but they were out-of-date. In fact, the puff of black smoke made by the powder in these cannons showed the Spanish exactly where to shoot. Every time the Americans fired, the Spanish took aim at the smoke.

But the Americans were determined — they would not turn from this battle. They had slowly grown more accustomed to the jungle. They must show the Spanish that they were in for a fight. Together, the 10,000 soldiers threw their gear aside. Either they would win and return for their belongings, or die and it would belong to the enemy. Later, Lieutenant John Pershing described this march as a time "when the minutes seemed like hours."

As the Americans struck out and marched toward the enemy, they put into practice a new American weapon: the balloon. Great things had been expected of this signal balloon. It was raised into the air with Lieutenant Colonel Derby in its basket. From there, it was hoped, he would be able to identify the enemy's location. But the balloon had little gas in it, and it barely floated above the treetops. It was little more than a signal to show the Spanish where the Americans were. But the Spanish feared it all the same. Suddenly, every Spanish musket and cannon was trained on the balloon. It came toppling to the earth, where Derby stepped out unhurt. The great weapon was useless.

Without help from the balloon, the American rush finally reached the San Juan River. From here they could see their enemy and fire up at the Spanish on San Juan Hill. But this also meant the Spanish were firing down at the Americans, a definite advantage. Artillery rained down. The few soldiers near the head of the line that made it back were severely hurt.

The effect on the Americans was disastrous. One officer wrote, "stumbling, hopping, limping men further shook up the raw troops . . . who stared at the ghastly parade in mute horror." Finally, the soldiers began to turn and flee. It was too much. There was little ammunition, and there seemed to be no plan for an attack. They were sitting ducks. Then, suddenly, there came a rattling, hail-like sound, amplified a thousand times. It was the Gatling guns. These guns were one of the Americans' strongest weapons. Able to fire hundreds of bullets each minute, these weapons led to the modern machine gun.

"The sound of the Gatlings, 'coffee grinders' we called 'em," one man wrote, "was the best sound I ever heard on a battlefield." With new hope, the Americans turned back and began up the hill. The Gatling's bullets tore through the air, into the hillside, and through the Spanish trenches. "Charge!" the general yelled.

The soldiers on horseback were the first to tear up the hill. They were known as Rough Riders. One galloped ahead of the others and leaped over a barbed-wire fence. When he saw that he was not being followed he turned his horse, jumped the barbed wire again, and taunted his soldiers. "What are you? Cowards?" This rider with the blue polka-dot handkerchief around his neck was no ordinary rider. He was Theodore Roosevelt. The last time we saw him he was sitting behind a desk in Washington, DC, as the U.S. Assistant Secretary of the Navy. But when the war began, he had resigned the post so that he would not miss the fight. The other Rough Riders followed him over the fence and up the hill.

"They came more like a howling mob than soldiers," an eyewitness reported, "brandishing rifles and waving swords . . . it was less charge than wild rush." The Rough Riders teamed with African-

Theodore Roosevelt and the Rough Riders

American members of the black cavalry to chase the Spanish off of the hill and back to town. African-American regiments had fought in the Civil War, but never had blacks fought alongside whites. General Pershing later wrote that in this war he saw a nation torn by the Civil War become one again. "White regiments, black regiments, regulars and the [college-educated] Rough Riders, representing the young manhood of North and South, all fighting together."

At last, San Juan Hill was free. The Americans had lost 550 soldiers in the fierce fighting there. But now the American guns had a clear shot at the Spanish stronghold in Santiago. In July, the U.S. Army met the U.S. Navy in Santiago. The Spanish had no choice. In late July, the Spanish surrendered at Santiago.

Newspaperman Hearst called this the "Splendid Little War." The American public seized this phrase. Later, Americans would come to view the Spanish-American War as one that need never have been fought. Pressed by the public, the government had consented to a senseless war. Through this war, American society learned a new respect for the power of the newspaper press. And overseas, the United States began to be seen as a force to be reckoned with, a country with international interests.

But one individual benefitted more than any other from the war with Spain. The tale of Teddy Roosevelt's brave charges at the head of his band of Rough Riders became national legend. Americans loved his brash, rough fighting spirit. He became a political celebrity. When McKinley was reelected in 1900, it was largely because Roosevelt would be his Vice-President. In 1901, McKinley was shot by an assassin's bullet and Teddy Roosevelt became the twenty-sixth President of the United States.

World War I
THE MEUSE-ARGONNE OFFENSIVE

The Spanish-American War had put the United States into the world arena. It had shown the world that the United States was powerful enough to try and affect world events. In political terminology, the United States had become a "major player" in buying and selling overseas, as well as in international diplomacy. Trade and relations of different sorts with other countries became commonplace. The United States began to be respected for its industry and culture. It also began constructing a powerful military to defend itself and the friends it was making throughout the world.

But as such a young country, the United States remained an outsider in many ways. Many of the European nations had been around for much longer than the United States. Some of these nations had long-standing rivalries with one another. During the late 1800's, the European nations had begun signing agreements or alliances with one another that divided the continent into sides. These agreements said that if one of the countries went to war, its allies would follow. Today, we know that such agreements can lead to World War, in which every nation is fighting for one side or the other. Then, leaders had no such ideas.

There were two main sets of alliances: the Triple Alliance, composed of Italy, Germany, and Austria-Hungary; and the Triple Entente, composed of Great Britain, France, and Russia. With all these agreements, one wrong move could throw the entire world into war. In 1914, an American diplomat described the situation to U.S. President Woodrow Wilson like this: "Everybody's nerves are tense. It only requires a spark to set the whole thing off." In June of that year, the spark flared. The Archduke of Austria, the heir to his country's throne, was assassinated by a man from the country of Serbia.

On July 28, 1914, Austria declared war on Serbia, which had close ties to Russia. Germany was afraid it would be caught between enemy nations, so it declared war on Russia and France. Great Britain felt it too must select a side. It declared war on Germany. Within a week, a small incident had grown into a global war. Over the next few years, all the powerful nations of the world would choose a side in the fighting.

In early September, President Wilson declared that the United States would remain neutral in the war. Over the next three years, the bloodiest fight-

President Woodrow Wilson

ing the world had ever seen swept through Europe. Americans had originally taken pride in their neutrality. "This was a European problem," they said. But the United States had close ties to both France and Great Britain. As news of the bloody fighting came back, Americans couldn't help but feel compassion for their friends.

But Wilson continued to stand by his vow of neutrality, lending U.S. money to both sides. With a war raging across the ocean, there was little doubt that Americans would be affected. The Germans were using their powerful submarine fleet to sink enemy vessels, as well as to stop commercial shipping into enemy countries. It was at this point that the British cruise liner *Lusitania* was sunk off of Ireland. Of the 1,198 people killed, 128 were Americans.

The New York Times.

EXTRA
5:30 A.M.

VOL. LXIV...NO. 20,933.   NEW YORK, SATURDAY, MAY 8, 1915—TWENTY-FOUR PAGES.   ONE CENT

LUSITANIA SUNK BY A SUBMARINE, PROBABLY 1,260 DEAD; TWICE TORPEDOED OFF IRISH COAST; SINKS IN 15 MINUTES; CAPT. TURNER SAVED, FROHMAN AND VANDERBILT MISSING; WASHINGTON BELIEVES THAT A GRAVE CRISIS IS AT HAND

SHOCKS THE PRESIDENT

Washington Deeply Stirred by the Loss of American Lives.

BULLETINS AT WHITE HOUSE

Wilson Reads Them Closely, but Is Silent on the Nation's Course.

HINTS OF CONGRESS CALL

Loss of Lusitania Recalls Firm Tone of Our First Warning to Germany.

CAPITAL FULL OF RUMORS

Reports That Liner Was to be Sunk Were Heard Before Actual News Came.

The Lost Cunard Steamship Lusitania
X Where the First Torpedo Struck.   XX Where the Second Torpedo Struck.

SOME DEAD TAKEN ASHORE

Several Hundred Survivors at Queenstown and Kinsale.

STEWARD TELLS OF DISASTER

One Torpedo Crashes Into the Doomed Liner's Bow. Another Into the Engine Room.

SHIP LISTS OVER TO PORT

Makes It Impossible to Lower Many Boats, So Hundreds Must Have Gone Down.

ATTACKED IN BROAD DAY

Only 650 Were Saved, Few Cabin Passengers

Canard Office Here Besieged for News; Fate of 1,918 on Lusitania Long in Doubt

List of Saved Includes Capt. Turner; Vanderbilt and Frohman Reported Lost

Saw the Submarine 100 Yards Off and Watched Torpedo as It Struck Ship

The sinking of the Lusitania

Many Americans began clamoring for war. "There is no question about going to war," said former President Theodore Roosevelt, who spoke for many Americans. "Germany is already at war with us!" But Germany hadn't declared war on the United States. After the sinking of the *Lusitania*, the Germans cut back drastically on their submarine warfare. But on March 16, 1917, the American ships *City of Memphis* and *Illinois* were torpedoed by German subs.

On April 2, Wilson appeared before Congress. He said: "There is one choice we cannot make, we are incapable of making: [we] will not choose the path of submission. The world must be made safe for democracy. Its peace must be founded on the trusted foundations of political liberty." Then

President Wilson asked Congress for a declaration of war against Germany. It came on April 6. America's years of isolation were over. For the first time in history, Americans were crossing the Atlantic to fight in a war among the great powers of the world! Americans celebrated by singing songs like "Over There." It told the Europeans to prepare, and say a prayer, for "The Yanks Are Coming!"

By this point in the war, both sides had suffered greatly. Supplies and manpower had run dangerously low for both. Like two battered and bruised prize fighters, the two sides now leaned against one another waiting to see who would make the next move. The entrance of the United States on the Allied side was a crushing blow to the German morale. The fresh resources and military of an entire nation would now be thrown at their tired soldiers. The same facts gave the Allies new energy. The Germans rushed into their fourth offensive of the war before the Americans arrived.

The first U.S. forces were mixed in with battalions from other nations. They helped stop this last German thrust. Then French Marshal Ferdinand Foch met with U.S. General John J. Pershing to plan the combined effort. The Allies would throw everything they had at their opponents. "Everyone," said Marshal Foch, "is to attack as soon as they can, as strong as they can, for as long as they can." It would be one of the greatest offensives of all time: twelve Allied armies would attack at once. We are no longer talking about

General John J. Pershing inspecting French troops

forces such as those used in American warfare up to this point. This assault would be made by over six million troops!

How could this many troops be organized under one battle plan? This was the first problem for the war planners to overcome. To prepare, Pershing's first task was to move over 600,000 Americans and 93,000 animals across France, to the Meuse-Argonne front. This would be the site of the attack.

Tanks rattled and snorted up to their jump-off positions. These weapons, painted in strange green, red, and brown patterns, were new to war.

These tanks were little like those used today. A British invention, tanks were designed to clear paths through barbed wire and wipe out machine gun nests ahead of advancing infantry. They were not offensive, attack weapons. *Tank* was the code word used to keep the weapon secret until its first use in 1916. In World War I, tanks were male or female. Male, or heavy tanks, carried machine guns and a small cannon; female tanks had only machine guns. Neither was very comfortable to be in. They bounced along on tractor treads, shaking their crews until their heads reeled. And the heat from the engine came right through, making them almost unbearably hot.

The Germans had stretched their forces across an incredibly wide area called the Hindenburg Line. This line was a series of defensive fortifications, the likes of which the world had never seen before. For the Allies to make it through just one stage would be a major accomplishment. To break completely through seemed impossible. The big offensive was scheduled to begin on September 26, 1917, with a massive American drive toward Sedan, a French city taken early in the war by Germany that had since been serving as an important German rail depot. The Allies would attempt to burst directly through this line.

General Pershing planned to rely on his aircraft to dominate the sky. Led by their ace, Eddie Rickenbacker, the U.S. pilots flew bravely in World War I, the first air combat of any war. The general knew he could count on them. The rest of Persh-

Eddie Rickenbacker, ace pilot

ing's plan was simply to overwhelm the oppo-
nent — his forces outnumbered the Germans
eight to one. But surprise was the main factor. All
the American troops scouting the area just prior
to the attack were dressed in French uniforms so
the Germans would not know the Americans had
arrived.

On each day after the main American attack
began, the French, British, and Belgians would
also make their own attacks. They were to hammer
away, ignoring losses, until they broke through the
Hindenburg Line. The main form of fighting was
called "trench warfare." Troops would dig long
gullies in the earth for protection — this was necessary because of the new weapons being used.

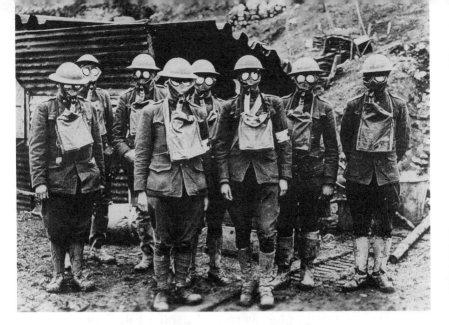

U.S. soldiers wearing gas masks

These new weapons made World War I different from any war before it. Military scientists had searched to devise new ways to kill men — guns no longer seemed enough. In addition to many types of guns, there were missiles, rockets, aircraft, and poison gases being used in battle. The thought of these weapons struck fear into every soldier. Especially the Americans, many of whom had only four months' worth of service — in some cases no more than six weeks!

In making its long journey, the American 1st Army marched only at night. Heavy rains had turned the dirt roads into streams of mud. Military policemen shouted themselves hoarse directing traffic over the din of sloshing boots and chugging motors. Smoking was forbidden, since glowing cigarettes were visible to enemy scout planes. Vehicle lights were painted over, except for a tiny square in the center covered with blue paper; without these specks of light, drivers wouldn't have been able to stay in line.

The center of each road was a jumble of trucks, rolling kitchens, water wagons, ambulances, tanks, cannon, and ammunition containers. From time to time there was a loud crash as a piece of heavy equipment skidded into a ditch. The column bunched up, remaining nearly motionless until the obstacle was removed. If it couldn't be righted quickly, it was heaved off the road and left for junk. Wagons and mules were still used a lot. Sweating mule "skinners" encouraged their animals with shouts and curses. Animals that slipped and broke a leg, or collapsed from fatigue, were shot and left behind. The troops could stop for nothing.

The infantry trudged along the roadsides where the mud was deepest. Some, their rifles slung over their shoulders, had loaves of bread skewered on their bayonets: they were too bulky to fit into backpacks and too precious to be left behind. As the first rays of sunlight purpled the horizon, the marching columns left the roads. During the day they slept in the dripping woods and ate cold "monkey meat," the name given to the beef rations the French supplied. Cooking fires might alert the enemy to the buildup, so everything was eaten cold and raw. By nightfall, when the march resumed, soldiers were already exhausted.

Despite these difficulties, the 1st Army reached its destination by the evening of September 25, 1918 — it stood ready to launch the Meuse-Argonne Offensive. The steep, wooded hillsides along the Meuse River and the plateau of the Argonne Forest were held by the enemy. A few seconds after midnight, September 25, four thousand guns opened fire on the German positions. Before they finished this initial bombardment, the Americans would drop forty thousand tons of shells on the Germans. This is more than all the cannon ammunition fired by the Union Army during the entire Civil War!

Around 5:00 A.M. the Yanks — Allied troops — started walking forward. The Germans were taken completely by surprise. For two days, their Hindenburg Line of troops gave ground steadily. The Allied troops were in high spirits and sang, "We'll hang out the washing on the old Hindenburg Line!" But after two days, the attack bogged down. A battle plan is an overall picture that outlines the duties of certain groups. The actual battle is never so orderly — particularly with so many troops from many different countries. This is where there is room for every soldier to become a hero or not. This is why there are so many great individual stories within a battle.

For instance, one battalion was ordered out to the western end of the Allied line. They were given the dangerous duty of seeing how far they could penetrate into the German lines. They would be far from the other troops, unable to get assistance if needed. This group would become known as "The Lost Battalion." The battalion advanced easily — too easily. After two days of little contact with the Germans, they found out why this had been the case. Suddenly, shells flew from all sides of their camp. They had been trapped, and were now surrounded.

The battalion bravely held off the Germans. But by the end of the first day, they knew what they were up against. They would be lucky to last another day. Their commander scribbled a message asking for food and artillery cover and attached it to the leg of a carrier pigeon. The bird flew to its coop near the U.S. headquarters. American outfits in the Argonne had no field telephones. All communications were written and carried by soldiers or on the tiny leg of a carrier pigeon.

The message arrived and the U.S. artillery came the next morning. But they had misread the note, and had the positions incorrect. Suddenly, The Lost Battalion found itself being shelled not only by the Germans, but also by its own American guns. The commander scribbled another note and attached it to the leg of Cher Ami, the battalion's last pigeon. The Germans tried to shoot the bird down, but it made it through. Cher Ami arrived at its loft with an eye gone, its breastbone shattered, and a leg shot away. But it delivered the important message.

The U.S. shelling stopped, but the Germans' continued. By the sixth day, the battalion was sure they had seen their last sunrise. With no more pigeons, three soldiers volunteered to take a final message. Two men returned; they had lost the third in the forest. It was impossible to break through, they said. Little did they know that the third man had gotten through the German line. The next morning, this soldier, Abe Krotoshinsky, brought reinforcements in the nick of time. His heroism saved the battalion. Of the 600 original members, 194 could walk out with their rescuers. Cher Ami, the hero pigeon, was given medals of honor and returned to the United States with a beautifully carved wooden leg. The stuffed bird is still on display in the Smithsonian Institution in Washington, DC.

In another battle, Sergeant Alvin C. York, a quiet, peace-loving man, refused to run for cover with his comrades when they stumbled upon German machine gunners. These guns were usually well hidden in high spots called "nests." In this particular nest, there were ten machine guns. Together, they could fire five thousand bullets every minute! York had only his rifle and his Tennessee hunting smarts. The Germans never had a chance. York finally returned to camp three hours later. He brought 132 German prisoners with him — taken single-handedly! York was given the Medal of Honor for his great courage.

Throughout October, the Meuse-Argonne Offensive continued. The Yanks advanced slowly, a series of battering rams smashing northward along

Sergeant Alvin C. York

parallel lines. On August 8, 1918, the Allies were poised to break completely through the Hindenburg Line. They had made it to the most difficult level of the German defenses. In an incredible stroke of luck, a prisoner taken on this day had the German maps for this portion of the line.

Using these maps, the Allies were able to design their plan of attack around the actual defenses laid out before them! The final push was led by a man destined to become a U.S. legend, Douglas MacArthur. Leading the Rainbow Division in a series of fierce head-on assaults, he stormed the last German stronghold. They were through! The

Meuse-Argonne campaign was over. The Yanks had lost 117,000 killed and wounded, but they had delivered the knockout blow. German morale cracked.

The German government accepted an armistice, based on President Woodrow Wilson's peace program. Known as the Fourteen Points, this program called for an end to secret treaties, for freedom of the seas, and the return of enemy-occupied territory. It also set up a League of Nations. Wilson wanted a world organization to abolish war by forcing nations to compromise their differences and to punish peace-breakers. The Armistice was signed on November 11, 1918. The war had been a terrible experience for everyone. From then on, World War I became known as "The War to End All Wars."

By waiting to join the war, the Americans had become the world's hero. They had made the difference in winning the war. World War I had also rallied the nation together. Most schools had gardens to help grow food for the troops. Every American rationed, or ate less, wheat products and meat so that more could be sent overseas. Every American was asked to buy "war bonds" to help finance the war effort. Most importantly, when nearly five million men had to leave and fight, women and those men who couldn't fight had to step up and fill in for them. It was the first time that many women had left the home to work. Now they were working on assembly lines, driving trucks, and performing many other jobs. During the war, U.S. industry showed itself to be the world leader in mass production. Rallying to the call of war, many American factories had made the weapons, jeeps, planes, tanks, and ships with incredible speed and efficiency. The war at home changed America forever, just as the war overseas had forever changed the world.

World War II
THE BATTLE OF MIDWAY

World War I had been referred to as "The War to End All Wars." The peace agreements made after that war were thought to insure a lasting world peace. However, in many ways, these agreements set the groundwork for the next global war. Germany was thrown into turmoil trying to fulfill the harsh limitations put on it after its defeat in World War I. This turmoil led to the single greatest factor in starting World War II. As Germany struggled to recover after the war, a group calling themselves Nazis were able to seize a great amount of power and survive the Great Depression. Leading this was a man named Adolf Hitler.

There were other factors: most notable was the worldwide disdain for another large war. When dictators took over Germany and Spain, European powers tended to look the other way. Dictators are leaders that wish to gain absolute control of a country. Often, they have a specific philosophy

Adolf Hitler

that their country must follow. Often, they wish to spread their philosophies to other countries, and are considered a great threat to neighboring nations.

Following World War I, the United States had completely isolated itself from the rest of the world. World War I had been a grave lesson for all. With the rest of the world afraid of another war in the late 1930's, Hitler saw an opportunity to spread his influence to other places. He was *not* afraid of war — it would be his tool for expanding his rule.

Hitler had two basic beliefs that he would pursue as the German leader. First, he believed that Germany needed more *Lebensraum*, or space for living. This space was to be found in eastern Europe. He believed Germany had the right to extend into the rest of Europe to find this needed space and construct its own empire. A strong military would clear the way for German dominance. Second, he believed one of the greatest obstacles to Germany achieving this goal was a single race of people. Hitler believed that Jewish people living in Germany and elsewhere had to be gotten rid of in order for Germany to rise to power.

Other European nations viewed Hitler's rise to power with alarm but also with uncertainty. It seemed impossible that he could ever have enough power to put these ideas into action. Part of the peace agreements following World War I was a strict restriction of arms to be made in Germany. However, soon after these agreements were made, it became obvious to all that Hitler was working furiously to give his nation the most powerful military in Europe. In 1938, Hitler's troops moved into Czechoslovakia. The other European nations criticized Germany, but refused to let this crisis grow into a larger war — they had learned their lesson in World War I.

One of the most alarmed nations was Germany's eastern neighbor, Poland, which had a large population of Jews. In 1934, Poland and Germany had signed a ten-year peace treaty and many believed that any problems had been eliminated. But in 1939, Germany demanded that Poland give up a section of land along the German border called the Danzig. In addition, they wanted the right to construct a railway across Polish territory to connect East Prussia with the rest of Germany. Poland refused, and Great Britain formally supported their refusal. It seemed as if war between Poland and Germany would break out at any moment.

Hitler waited all summer for a good cause to begin his campaign. On August 31, 1939, Hitler reported that Polish soldiers had attacked a German radio station on the Polish frontier near the German border. It was later discovered that the attackers were Germans dressed in Polish uniforms acting on orders from Hitler. They had been ordered to attack their own people in order to begin a large-scale war between these two countries. Hitler used this as his excuse. On September 1, German forces invaded Poland. Two days later, Great Britain and France declared war on Germany. The United States stated that this was a European problem, and declared its neutrality. But World War II had begun.

The war with Poland was over September 27. The German method of attack, called *Blitzkrieg*, was overwhelming in its force and cruelty. Tanks, planes, and troops completely leveled anything in their paths. British and French forces had formulated their own battle plans. All of these were defensive plans, awaiting German attack. The Germans drove through Belgium and into Paris, France, in early May and June, 1940. Italy then joined the German forces by declaring war on Great Britain and France.

With France defeated by 1940, Britain now stood alone. Britain drove back early German attacks. The U.S. Congress passed the Lend-Lease

Act in March of 1941, allowing the country to stay out of the actual fighting, but to give weapons and supplies to all nations fighting against the Axis powers. The United States supplied the Allied powers with billions of dollars worth of arms and services, but continued to proclaim its neutrality. In June of 1941, Germany attacked the powerful Soviet army, bringing the British a strong ally. Hitler was getting desperately near to his dream of ruling all of Europe.

Meanwhile, tensions were also growing in the Pacific region. In September, 1940, Japan signed on with the Axis powers, which were fighting along with Germany. Japan and Germany had similar goals, but were interested in separate parts of the world.

Early on Sunday morning, December 7, 1941, the bulk of the U.S. Pacific Navy fleet was moored in Pearl Harbor in the Hawaiian Islands, the largest U.S. Navy base. For a long time there had been speculation that Japan was interested in creating its own empire. This scared many Americans. However, with all attention focused on the fighting in Europe, little attention was being paid to any Japanese threat. That morning changed all this.

Japanese fighter planes, called Zeroes, descended on the completely unsuspecting Hawaiian community. When air-raid sirens first went off at Pearl Harbor, most Americans thought it was a drill. "This is no drill," boomed a voice over the loudspeaker. But that became obvious very quickly. The Japanese bombing killed 2,335 U.S.

The Japanese attack on Pearl Harbor

military personnel and left the portion of the U.S. Navy that was in charge of policing the Pacific Ocean out of action. For the Japanese, their plan to neutralize the United States had gone perfectly.

Never before in modern history had there been an attack upon American soil. The entire nation was up in arms. After World War I, the United States had no stomach for war. This had been the reason for instituting the Lend-Lease policy rather than sending troops to Europe. Now, war fever swept the United States. Americans were enraged! When British Prime Minister Winston Churchill telephoned U.S. President Franklin D. Roosevelt after hearing the news, Roosevelt's words were, "We are all in the same boat now." Within twenty-four hours, Roosevelt stood before Congress and said these words:

> Yesterday, December 7, 1941 — a date which will live in infamy — the United States of America was suddenly and deliberately attacked by naval and air forces of the Empire of Japan. . . . Very many American lives have been lost. Always will our whole nation remember the character of the onslaught against us. . . . No matter how long it may take to overcome this . . . invasion, the American people in their righteous might will win . . . absolute victory. We will not only defend ourselves to the uttermost but will make it very certain that this form of treachery shall never again endanger us. We will gain the inevitable triumph — so help us God. I ask that the Congress declare . . . a state of war.

The neutrality of the United States was thrown out the window. The United States had officially entered World War II. The attack on American soil had filled the entire nation with outrage. All Japanese-Americans were placed in prison camps. Officials feared they might commit terrorist acts inside the United States. War, for the first time, had hit Americans at home.

President Franklin D. Roosevelt signing the Declaration of War

Japanese aircraft carriers, navy ships, and Zeroes systematically began taking over the islands separating them from the United States. Victory after victory came for the fine Japanese flyers. Japanese warriors became completely overcome by "victory fever." They felt they could gain control of all the land they would ever need. The only nation in their path was the United States. In the Pacific region, whoever controls the sea controls the land. Admiral Chester Nimitz and the remaining U.S. Navy was all that stood between Japan's Admiral Yamamoto and control of the Pacific.

In early April, 1942, Japanese planners considered their options: to fight defensively and let the enemy come to them, or to attack the United States again.

On April 18, the U.S. aircraft carrier *Hornet* launched bombers which flew over Japan, bombing Tokyo and other cities. It was a show of force to the Japanese — proving that the United States was also willing *and* able to fight. For the Japanese, the decision of what to do next was suddenly made easier. Their task would be to rid the Pacific of the *Hornet* and all other United States carriers, and then consider moving inland. San Francisco and Alaska were discussed as possible invasion sites.

Aircraft carriers were coming of age in 1942. The fighting in the Pacific was tailor-made for carriers. The U.S. Navy was down to only 11 carriers compared with Japan's much stronger navy. But the war was already being fought in many other ways, too. One of the most startling was the use of "intelligence." In previous U.S. wars, spies had been used on both sides. However, never before had intelligence sources been as important as they would be in the next few months.

The intelligence center for the Navy's Pacific fleet was called Hypo or the Black Chamber. Sunlight never penetrates this basement office on the Navy Base on Oahu, Hawaiian Islands. Barred doors and armed guards prevent any secrets from escaping.

Throughout the war, both sides used many codes to send radio messages. These codes kept the enemy from understanding the messages that were being sent. Hypo had broken the Japanese code (code-named JN-25) in early 1940. This meant that they could now understand the intercepted Japanese transmissions. This was Hypo's greatest secret. If the Japanese ever found out that the United States understood JN-25, they would, of course, stop using it. The U.S. advantage would be gone.

In early May, two U.S. aircraft carriers battled two Japanese carriers. Naval history was made as the ships did battle without exchanging gunfire. Instead, planes from each ship scored damaging blows against their enemy's ships. Never before had a naval battle been fought solely by planes. Torpedo planes and bombers flew toward the enemy carrier escorted by fighter planes. Many times, they passed the enemy's own attack force on their way. Always, shots were held, as each group of planes continued to its target.

When each group attacked the carrier, fighter planes guarding the carrier would engage the approaching fighter planes. If the defenders overwhelmed the fighters, they could then shoot down the larger and slower torpedo planes and bombers, whose purpose is to attack the carriers themselves. The planes still flying after the fighting return to their own home carrier. But in these battles, many planes were shot down, never to return.

The U.S. carrier *Lexington* was sunk in the May 8, 1942 battle. The other U.S. carrier, *Yorktown*, was badly damaged and limped back to port for repairs. With two U.S. carriers out of service, the time was ripe for another Japanese attack. Earlier, on May 6, Hypo had intercepted word of a planned Japanese campaign. The location was given in a separate code as *AF*. By piecing together the code names for sites of previous attacks, Hypo came up with the location of the attack: Midway Island. To make sure, U.S. radio sent a dummy message over the public lines: *Midway is low on fresh water supplies*. Moments later they intercepted a JN-25 transmission: "*AF* is low on fresh water." This would be the site of the next Japanese attack!

Work on *Yorktown* was stepped up to prepare it for the battle — three weeks of work had to be completed in three days. *Yorktown* was to meet two other U.S. carriers, *Hornet* and *Enterprise* off Midway. Midway Island is a member of the Hawaiian chain, but it is little more than a desert island — without even one palm tree. Practically the only thing on the island is a U.S. air field.

Notified of an upcoming Japanese attack, all troops on Midway had built trenches, and extra planes, supplies, and troops had been flown in. Japanese submarines off the island's coast noted the increase in activity, but the Japanese leaders still believed they were about to catch the Americans completely off guard. Control of this island would mean clear sailing through the Pacific for the Japanese.

Early on June 3, 1942, an observation flight out of Midway spotted the Japanese ships. Immediately, planes from Midway took off to confront the enemy. The ships' antiaircraft guns teamed with the Zeroes to make quick work of the U.S. planes. All were shot down, and no hits were scored on the Japanese ships. Now, the Japanese leaders believed they had defeated all the U.S planes available. At 2:00 A.M., June 4, 1942, pilots were awakened on board the U.S. carriers that were now in position. They took their places in the situation room. Here they sat in full gear, being kept abreast of the battle, and waited for their call to action. Their time was near at hand.

At 4:25 A.M., the four Japanese carriers in the area ordered their pilots to their planes. The planes were soon in the air. At about the same time, bombers from *Yorktown* were sent out to locate the enemy carriers. On the way, they passed the Japanese planes traveling to Midway. The best time to attack the Japanese carriers was just after these planes returned, while there was confusion on deck and only a few planes ready to fly. It seemed odd to leave the Zeroes alone to attack their own base, but the American pilots knew their time would come.

At 6:00 A.M., the sirens on Midway began to howl. The approaching Zeroes downed nearly every American plane put in the air against them. At 6:31, the attack on the Midway base began. The raids lasted less than twenty minutes, but the U.S. base was left in smoke and debris.

Around 7:00 A.M., planes were sent out from *Hornet* and *Enterprise*. The Japanese still had no idea that U.S. carriers were nearby; they still believed that *Yorktown* had never completed its repairs and remained in dry dock! Soon, Japanese search planes gave their commanders the first in a series of shocks. They located a convoy of eleven American ships — but no carriers. The Japanese skippers were confused. Their planes were already being fitted with land bombs to finish off Midway. Should they be refitted with torpedoes to take on the U.S. ships? They were ordered to attack the ships with whatever bombs they already had on them. Five minutes later, the second shock came: the U.S. ships were accompanied by one carrier.

The Japanese planes returned from their bombing runs on Midway. A frenzy of activity began as the planes were fitted with torpedoes to attack the U.S. carrier. The Japanese commanders confidently radioed that the enemy would be destroyed within two hours. But before the Japanese planes could be readied, the planes from the U.S. carriers arrived. There was no real coordination between the pilots from the different U.S. ships, and the American planes were hit hard by the Zeroes patrolling the skies. A few U.S. planes survived long enough to drop torpedoes. Then, more and more American planes arrived. The Japanese commanders couldn't help but wonder from where so many planes were coming.

At 10:20 A.M., the Japanese were still about ten minutes from being able to launch their strike against the American ships. The gas lines used to fuel the planes lay scattered along the carriers' decks. Just as the launch order was being given, another group of U.S. planes descended on the Japanese carriers. Bomb after bomb rained down on the Japanese ships. Bombs and fuel lines on their decks ignited, causing a chain reaction of explosions throughout the ships. Away from the fighting, Admiral Yamamoto read a message that he expected would bring good news of victory. Instead, it read: "Fires raging aboard [three carriers] from attacks by enemy carrier. . . . We are temporarily withdrawing to the north to assemble our forces."

The Japanese struck back with their last swing. A few planes were able to break through defenses and bomb *Yorktown*. Though none of the blows were fatal, fires burned deep within the U.S. carrier. Finally, it was abandoned — but not before its pilots claimed a fourth Japanese carrier. The Japanese ships that were still operational turned and fled. That is, except for one beneath the surface. A Japanese submarine fired the last shots of the Battle of Midway Island, using three torpedoes to send the crippled and abandoned *Yorktown* to the ocean bottom. The Japanese didn't realize until later that they had actually been fighting the combined forces of three U.S. carriers!

The most important naval battle of the Pacific War left the Japanese crushed. Their offensive strategy was abandoned. They could no longer hope to complete an invasion of the United States. The tide of the Pacific fighting had swung toward the United States and would never swing away.

At home, Americans were thrilled. But there was still more war to be fought. Just as in World War I, the home front rallied behind their troops. Groups who were having difficulty getting work, such as African-Americans, Hispanic-Americans, and women, were once again responsible for keeping America going. Industry was once again shifted to war-time production of supplies for the troops.

"Victory Gardens" cropped up all over the country to grow produce to send to the troops. And once again, Americans bought war bonds; these bonds actually meant that they were lending money to the government. With every scrap of metal important, recycling efforts collected anything from toothpaste tubes to tin cans. Sugar, coffee, tires, gasoline, nylon, and shoes were all rationed in the United States so that there would be enough to send overseas. With a shortage of socks in the U.S. Army, many Americans even knitted socks and sent them to Europe! The slogan for America became, "Use it up, wear it out, make it do, or do without."

World War II
D-DAY

With the Japanese Navy weakened, the immediate threat to the United States was gone. Now, the American battle planners could concentrate fully on helping the Allies defeat the German Nazis in Europe. This task would not be easy. Adolf Hitler's troops had proven to be some of the toughest the world had ever seen. Young men raised from their youth to be good soldiers, these Nazis did whatever their *Führer*, or ruler, asked. The things this madman had asked of his soldiers haunt every human being to this day.

As you read in the last chapter, Hitler believed that the Jews would keep the Germans from attaining success. Hitler believed in the strength of the "pure" Germans. He felt the Jews and other groups living in Germany pulled down what he called the great German, "master" race. Upon seizing power, Hitler began an incredible plan to rid Germany and, possibly, the whole world of Jews.

105

It sounds crazy now, and it was crazy then. But what became known as the Holocaust is absolute truth.

Hitler had his Nazi soldiers destroy the homes and businesses of Jews. He made life miserable for Jews, hoping to force them to leave Germany. Many did leave, but many more could not. As World War II neared, most nations refused to accept more Jews from Germany. Hitler ordered all the remaining Jews in Germany to be put into prison camps. The Nazis used a senseless system in the camps to try to rob prisoners of their dignity. These former business owners, workers, and children were forced to perform such jobs as moving a pile of sand between two points all day. When Hitler began his attack on Poland, he also began discussing his ideas for a "Final Solution" to rid Germany of Jews. Nearly two years later, the first death camps would be built in order to carry out his "Final Solution."

Jews in the camps were killed by the thousands. Shot or poisoned in gas chambers, the dead were then heaped into open pits. There was no mercy shown. By the winter of 1941–42, 90 percent of the Jews living in Germany and in invaded portions of Russia had been killed. By the time the war ended in 1945, the Nazis had killed six million Jews — one half of all the Jews in Europe — and another six million people of other, "lesser" races. The world had never seen anything like it.

On the battle front, the Nazi offensive had been

long and strong. The Axis powers of Germany and Italy had struck fear into all the world. The German army took over Denmark and Norway while closing in on France. The Nazi troops then moved through Belgium and into France. By June, 1940, France had fallen under Nazi control.

This was the situation facing the United States and its Allies. German planners set out to prepare for an Allied offensive to retake France. They believed it made the most sense for Allied divisions to attack in the Pas-de-Calais area. The Allied Navy furthered this belief with naval demonstrations off the Channel coast. They would make the Germans believe they would attack here, but they would go elsewhere.

Now the big question became obvious: How can you attack when you have no weapons or bases in the area in which you wish to fight? The Germans controlled all of France. Everything the Allies needed to force the Germans from France had to be brought by boat or plane and landed on the coast. However, the Germans also controlled the coast. The Allies had to first try to change this.

On May 8, 1944, U.S. General Dwight Eisenhower designated D-Day or the Battle of Normandy as June 5, 1944. American, British, and Canadian forces would storm fifty miles of the coast of Normandy in German-occupied France. It would be the largest amphibious assault of all time. For this reason, everything depended on the weather. On June 4, bad weather caused Eisen-

General Dwight D. Eisenhower reviewing his troops

hower, or Ike as he was known, to postpone the invasion to June 6.

Two beaches along the French coast were the American targets. Over 120,000 men and over 12,000 vehicles would go ashore at Omaha and Utah beaches on the morning of June 6. All of these troops and vehicles would have to be brought ashore by boat. Landing crafts, which had no seats and were more like barges, could carry thirty-two soldiers within a few yards of the shore. Tanks and other equipment were outfitted with special floats that would carry them near the shore. On that morning, over 4,000 ships and other craft crashed the shores.

The danger was incredible. Even though they did not expect the attack here, German troops were well dug in along the beaches. Tanks and other artillery combined with many machine-gun nests to defend the French coast. As if that weren't enough, a message was rushed to the American troops at the last minute. It read:

Flooded areas back of the beaches are over a man's head in places because before the enemy blocked the streams, bulldozers plowed furrows in the meadows. . . . The enemy may spread oil on the marshes, and if there is a landing, the oil will be set afire.

The idea of flaming marshes filled the troops with terror — particularly those who would be first ashore. No matter how many soldiers take part in an attack from sea, some must be the first ashore. These soldiers would be completely helpless during the moments when they left their boats and waded ashore. They knew these German soldiers would stop at nothing. The final message to the troops was simple: "The time has come to deal the enemy a terrific blow in Western Europe."

Each soldier was outfitted with a self-inflating life preserver for the approach in the surf and the marshes. But there would be no defense against the fire. Each soldier also had to struggle to remain afloat with heavy burdens of artillery, guns, and other supplies. As they approached the shore,

American troops and supply vehicles arriving on the French coast in the D-Day invasion

many of the first invading troops were shot by German machine gunners. But there were no flaming marshes and, slowly, the Allies pushed on.

Paratroopers were dropped behind enemy lines, so that the attack would come from two sides. They were dropped at night, when it was difficult to distinguish who was a German and who was not. In order to help these troops distinguish friend from foe, thousands of mechanical crickets were distributed. As one of the paratroopers approached another figure in the night, he held his gun in one hand and would snap his mechanical cricket with the other. If the *crick-crack* answer came back, all was well. If not, weapons were used.

The initial phases of the attack went well, but then there was a standstill. At certain beaches, the soldiers who made it ashore found themselves at the base of huge cliffs. Atop these cliffs were the German guns killing many of the invading Allies. They had to be stopped. To reach them, soldiers used their bayonets to climb the cliffs. They would drive the blade into a crevice between the rocks and pull themselves up a few feet. They repeated this till they finally reached the top. There were other problems. The Germans had buried small, saucer-shaped mines all along the cliffs and beaches. The slightest touch set off these explosives. The going was slow. Once on top, the soldiers then had to overpower the Germans manning the guns. Then they would drop ropes to help the oncoming troops climb.

There were heavy losses, but the storming of the Normandy coast was a success. Hitler no longer controlled the beaches. It was time to bring in the supplies to drive him out of France! To do this, the Allies unveiled one of military history's greatest engineering feats: a prefab dock had been constructed in pieces and was now put together on the French coast. A huge structure made of steel girders, this dock was welded together in hours. Now, supplies could be unloaded easily. Within three weeks, almost one million troops, 500,000 tons of supplies, and 177,000 vehicles had been landed in the zones now controlled by British and American forces. The necessary items for war were in place. It was time for the Allies to take the offensive.

Getting the Allied troops safely onto French soil had been the turning point of World War II. But now the troops had to push their advantage. Even though the tide had shifted, there was still hard work to be done. U.S. General Omar Bradley led the attack as Allied forces pressed inland from their spots on the French coast. On July 25, Operation Cobra got underway as 2,500 Allied planes carpet-bombed German positions. (In this type of bombing, areas are divided into rectangles which are thoroughly bombed. There is no specific site in mind.) American troops followed on foot. It was not until the third day of fighting that Bradley's men achieved the first large break in the German line. Over the next month, these troops would continue to drive through France. By late August, and after many great battles, the Allies had nearly reached Paris. Many officials believed this would be the greatest challenge.

Like a boxer, the Allies had their enemies on the ropes. But the Nazis could still inflict damage. Any battle to retake Paris would surely ruin the beauty and history of this great city. The Allies debated whether or not they could take the city without a battle. Meanwhile, Hitler had told his military leaders holding Paris that the city was a fortress for which they should fight long and hard. Even if he lost France, to control Paris was still a triumph because of the city's prestige. A kind of standoff ensued. Eisenhower decided the Allies could wait no longer. He revised his plans and began preparing for the battle to win Paris.

General Omar Bradley

When the Parisians heard of the standoff, they decided to take matters into their own hands. Since the German invasion of France, the French people had been forced to live under Nazi occupation. When the French heard through their underground newspapers that their liberation — or freedom — from the Nazis was near, they decided to try to save their city from a battle. They would take it back themselves! They paraded through the streets, waving French flags. Millions of French citizens, young and old, took to the streets. The Germans were overwhelmed.

Lacking a means to put down the uprising in the face of surrounding Allied troops, Hitler ordered his troops to withdraw. But first, he ordered them to set fire to the city. If he couldn't have Paris, no one would! But as the Nazis began to set fires, Allied troops arrived. The Nazis fled from the city. Paris was free! Parisians held great celebrations, and thanked every Allied soldier they could find.

This was the beginning of the end for the German army. Beginning in early 1945, Soviet, British, American, and French forces began squeezing Germany in a gigantic vise. Soon, every German but Hitler knew the war was lost. Then, on April 30, 1945, Hitler — one of the most evil men the world has ever produced — committed suicide. On May 7, 1945, the war against the Germans ended. The next day, V-E Day (meaning Victory in Europe) celebrated the end of the war that had raged for five years.

President Franklin Roosevelt, British Prime Minister Winston Churchill, and Soviet leader Joseph Stalin had been the backbone that held the Allies together. But Roosevelt didn't get to see this day. He died earlier in 1945. His Vice-President, Harry S. Truman, signed the peace agreements with Germany. That, however, was the easy part. Truman also had to rally the Allies and the American people to their next and final challenge. Don't forget, the Japanese army still had not been defeated!

The Japanese would not surrender easily. Faced with the thought of more fighting, which would certainly cost the Allies many more lives, Truman made one of the most important decisions in world history. Truman chose in early August, 1945, to

114

use a new weapon to stop the war with Japan. Germany and the United States had been racing against each other to perfect the world's first atomic bomb. Through a sudden burst of atomic energy, these bombs would exert many times the energy of other bombs — but no one was sure how much damage they would truly inflict on an actual city.

The United States had paid nearly $2.5 billion for a three-year project known as the Manhattan Project. With the first successful testing of the bomb on July 16, 1945, the United States had won the race. One week later, Truman decided the atomic bomb was the only way to end the war quickly. He reasoned that countless American lives would be saved.

Leaflets dropped in Japan on August 5 read: "Your city will be obliterated unless your government surrenders." Rumors of America's new bomb had spread throughout the world. But no one knew what to expect. Could it really be powerful enough to "obliterate" an entire city?

No Japanese surrender was forthcoming, so less than a month after its first successful testing, an American plane, *Enola Gay*, dropped the world's first atomic bomb on the Japanese city of Hiroshima. One of the pilots later reported that "it looked as if the entire city had been torn apart." An eyewitness described the scene: "A lightning flash covered the whole sky. . . . All [that was] green . . . perished."

After the initial explosion, radiation infected any

human or other living creature within miles. Radioactive rain that burned human skin fell from the sky — one Japanese cried, "They are dropping gasoline on us!" The city was leveled, and 78,000 Japanese were killed. Truman explained what had occurred to Americans:

> Sixteen hours ago an American airplane dropped one bomb on Hiroshima . . . [with] more power than 20,000 tons of TNT. . . . If they do not now accept our [peace] terms, they may expect a rain of ruin from the sky the likes of which has never been seen on this earth.

Ground crew of the Enola Gay, *which dropped the atomic bomb on Hiroshima*

Today, many people wonder how the United States could inflict such pain and suffering on Japanese civilians. But the United States of 1945 was different from that of today. The attack on Pearl Harbor had filled the Americans with more rage than anyone had ever thought possible. This attack had pulled the country into a war in which it did not wish to participate. The ensuing years of war had cost a generation of men and billions of dollars. The only reason for the war had been the interest of two nations in gaining more power. The idea of being able to end the war with no more American deaths seemed too good to be true.

Three days later, planes dropped another atomic bomb on Nagasaki. Forty thousand more Japanese were killed. The Japanese emperor ordered his military leaders to surrender and a ceasefire was declared on August 15. The Japanese formally surrendered on September 2, V-J Day. World War II was over. All of Europe would be divided between the victorious Allied powers. It would change the look of the globe for many years to come.

The Korean War
INCHON LANDING

Americans have watched the news of the restructuring of the Soviet Union with great interest in recent years. Today, the former Soviet Union is known as the Commonwealth of Independent States. But after World War II, the Soviet Union and the United States were the only two nations considered world superpowers. If this weren't enough to make them enemies, their differing philosophies were.

The former Soviet Union's power had come from a philosophy known as communism. Under this new form of government, Russia began linking many separate nations together to form the Soviet Union. Russia became one of the many republics in the Soviet Union. The Soviets began taking over neighbors by force in order to protect themselves from another attack from the West. But soon, the United States and other democratic nations stopped believing that the Soviets were only trying to protect themselves; in fact, the Soviets were trying to spread communism throughout the world — by force.

In a communist society, factories, newspapers, and other businesses are controlled by the government. The Soviet government oversaw all of this in every one of its republics. The money and products created by industry all belonged to the central government. People living under communism are not free to choose things such as jobs, places to live, or even when to take a vacation. In communist countries, there is no free trade such as in the United States. The government owns everything, and is supposed to use the profits to run the country. The United States is run as a democracy, where people can do as they please — within the bounds of laws.

From 1950 onward, the Soviet Union and the United States were constantly at odds because of their differing beliefs and principles. During this era, the two countries were said to be in a state of "Cold War." Each country felt a constant threat from the other. The United States constantly suspected the Soviets of trying to expand communism. The Soviets constantly suspected the United States of preventing nations from choosing their own form of government — particularly when that form would be communism.

This conflict led the United States to set up military bases in many small countries to the south of the Soviet Union. By setting up bases in countries such as South Korea, the United States hoped

119

to stop the spread of communism. This practice became known as containment. American bases were placed in friendly countries on which the United States thought the Soviets may have designs.

Another aspect of the Cold War came out of that single bomb dropped from *Enola Gay*. Until 1949, the United States had unlimited world power because it alone had nuclear weapons. But in 1949, the United States received reports that it no longer held the nuclear trump card. The Soviets had perfected their own nuclear weapon. This led to great competition between the United States and the Soviet Union. This arms buildup saw both the United States and the Soviet Union make enough nuclear missiles to destroy each other many times over. However, each country still tried to develop more advanced weapons, or at least to make *more* missiles than the other.

These missiles were often put in stategic friendly nations near the enemy country. People in both countries lived in constant fear of an attack by the other. During the 1950's, children all over the United States had "duck and cover" drills — just like fire drills — that showed them what to do in case of a nuclear attack. But with the two great powers at a standoff, officials in both countries mostly feared that a conflict over another, smaller country could heat up the Cold War and trigger World War III — the first complete nuclear war.

Late on the night of June 25, 1950, U.S. Presi-

President Harry S. Truman and General Douglas MacArthur

dent Harry Truman was awoken while on vacation in Missouri. The voice on the other end of the phone informed him that the Republic of Korea had been invaded by a force from the north. Truman realized this news was bad. In many ways, the situation was worse than those leading up to previous wars. This situation was highly complicated. He would have to be very careful if the United States were going to keep this from growing into World War III.

"Why does Korea matter so much?" you may ask. So did many Americans on the morning of June 26. But Korea did matter greatly. After living under Japanese rule, Korea was to be set free after the Japanese were defeated in World War II. The Koreans celebrated, and the Allies made plans to hold elections to bring the Republic of Korea into existence. The new country would have the same boundaries it had before the Japanese invasion.

But this was not to be. The Soviet Union and the United States, who had fought as allies in World War II, agreed to divide Korea in half. What the American government regarded as a temporary military arrangement, the Soviets regarded as the permanent division of Korea into two nations: a Communist North and a non-Communist South. The United States handed the problem over to the United Nations (UN), but little action could be taken.

Koreans spoke the same language, held the same traditions, and lived on the same peninsula, but were two separate countries. Even more unfortunate, most Koreans lived in the South, while most of the industry, as well as rice and other food, was produced in the North. There was only a slim border separating them, but it may as well have been a million miles wide. The Soviet Union and the UN controlled Korea's fate — Koreans had little to say in the matter. And now North and South Koreans had to live with the constant threat of war. If you consult an atlas, you will see that North Korea shares a border with the former Soviet Union and with China, another communist nation, which also bordered the Soviet Union. There was nothing to keep these strong, Communist powers from invading South Korea and uniting Korea into one Communist country.

The UN arranged for elections in North and South Korea, but the Soviets refused to allow elections in the North. The UN elections in 1948 set up the Republic of Korea, a country about the size of the state of Virginia. The Soviets set up the People's Democratic Republic of Korea shortly thereafter. The South Koreans looked to the United States for diplomatic help in *reuniting* their country. The North Koreans looked to China and the Soviet Union to help give them a strong enough military to *take over* all of the peninsula. The sole purpose of this powerful North Korean army was the invasion of South Korea. And that is exactly what happened on June 25, 1950, when 90,000 Communist soldiers swept over the border.

While President Truman returned to Washington, DC, to begin planning the next American move, the UN was organizing support at its headquarters in New York. It called for a cease-fire and Communist withdrawal. The UN asked its members to lend support to South Korea. Both as a member of the UN and as protector of the Republic of Korea, the United States took a leading role in halting the invasion. Planes and ships began bombing the invading troops. It was a grave step. Would the Soviets and Chinese assist the North Koreans and expand the war? It was hoped that having the UN on its side would help the South Koreans and the United States.

One of the greatest generals in American history was already overseeing U.S. forces in the Far East. General Douglas MacArthur, who had gained a reputation for guts and blind courage during World War II, took over as head of the UN forces.

Within three days, Seoul — the capital of the Republic of Korea — was taken by the Communists. President Truman authorized MacArthur to order in American ground troops. The call went out to bases throughout the United States. America was at war — *kind of*.

In order to maintain its status as an international power, the United States believed it needed to stop the spread of the Soviet Union and communism. But without an attack on the United States itself, was an all-out war justified? Politicians asked this question, and they knew every American would also wonder. Would the American people be willing to sacrifice the money and lives needed to help a far-off friend? Officials in the United States weren't sure.

The Korean War would become the first "partial" war in U.S. history. President Truman did not ask Congress for a declaration of war. Many historians believe he was afraid he might not get it. Instead, he called the U.S. involvement in Korea a "police action." The Korean War lasted for three years, but war was never officially declared! This war would be fought as much through diplomacy as through military attacks. While soldiers manned the battlefield, diplomats met to try to work out a solution.

President Truman hoped that the conflict could be solved through diplomacy — not war. But first, the communist invasion had to be stopped. It was a delicate situation. And many historians feel that, as great a leader as he was, General MacArthur was the wrong man for this job. MacArthur knew only all-out war. Years later, this is how MacArthur described his views:

> I know war as few other men now living know it, and nothing, to me, is more revolting. . . . But once war is forced upon us, there is no alternative than to apply every available means to bring it to a swift end. . . . War's very object is victory.

Once a war started, MacArthur wanted to end it as soon as possible — no fooling around. But due to the ongoing diplomacy, the Korean War could not be an all-out war. An all-out war in Korea would almost surely lead to World War III.

The Korean War was a frustrating experience for General MacArthur. But there was no better leader for the United States during the next few months. His orders were simple: stop the Communist invasion. The UN troops tried to dig in as the Communists approached. Constantly pushed back, UN forces finally were driven to Pusan at the southern tip of South Korea. There was only ocean behind them! U.S. General Walton H. Walker ordered the retreat to stop — there was nowhere to go.

> There will be no more retreating, withdrawal, readjustment of lines or whatever else you call it. There are no lines behind which we can retreat. . . . We must fight

until the end. We must fight as a team. If some of us must die, we will die fighting together.

The UN forces rallied and the invasion was stopped. But the real fight had just begun.

MacArthur now had to come up with a plan to get the Communists out of South Korea. To do this, he planned what military experts describe as one of the most brilliant military campaigns in history. But, at the time, his own officers described it as having only a 5,000-to-one chance of working.

General MacArthur's plan called for troops to make an amphibious assault — such as the storming of the Normandy beach on D-Day in World War II. The United States-led UN forces would

Military observers of the United Nations looking over a map of artillery positions in Korea

come in behind the North Koreans in a surprise attack. Before dawn on September 15, 1950, British and American ships began to shell the Communist troops along the coast. Planes also dropped bombs filled with napalm, a poisonous jellylike chemical, on the Communist troops.

MacArthur's 5,000-to-one plan would have troops soon landing on the shores of South Korea. But this is when the riskiest part of the plan came into play. This was no ordinary beach. This was the Inchon Harbor, where the tide changes are the most dangerous in the world. The tides rise and fall thirty feet in a matter of minutes! At any beach, you've probably seen how the ocean comes up farther at high tide. But in Inchon, when the tide goes out, the bay becomes a vast, three-mile long mud flat. Ships could be stuck in the muddy bottom, or soldiers drowned in the flood — all sitting ducks for the enemy. These were problems, but they also were why MacArthur wanted to attack at Inchon: the Communists would never expect an attack from here, because they also would think it was impossible!

The landing crafts moved into position, and a few Marines were sent in to shore first. One of these, a young naval Lieutenant named Eugene Clark, had landed on September 1 in order to prepare the beach for the invasion. What he did at that time is given credit for the success of the Inchon Landing. After accomplishing his assigned tasks, Clark climbed up to the lighthouse looking out over the harbor. The light had been off throughout the war. Now, he threw the switch. The invading UN troops were able to use the light that swept by every forty seconds as a guide to shore!

At exactly high tide, landing craft entered the narrow channel. For the first time in naval history, airplanes flew low over the beach, their machine guns sputtering at the defenders. Troops streamed on to land at top speed. By the time the tide rushed out, an entire army had been put ashore. The North Koreans were caught completely by surprise. The American-led UN forces quickly controlled the port and moved north. MacArthur sent these words to the troops: "The Navy and Marines have never shone more brightly than this morning." Soon, Seoul was recaptured.

Marines landing at the Inchon invasion

The North Koreans were completely separated from their supplies. Now, the rest of the UN army moved up from their position in the South. The North Koreans were trapped between this army and MacArthur's Marines at Inchon. The North Koreans fell apart, and more than 100,000 troops were taken prisoner. The invasion had been stopped. The landing at Inchon was a great success.

MacArthur saw this as a terrific opportunity. He took his troops and moved North, over the border into North Korea. First, he captured the North Korean capital, then he continued to move toward the Chinese border. There was tension in Washington. The Chinese would grow uneasy with an enemy force so near its border. MacArthur was ordered to halt at the Yalu River. Only South Korean troops could advance farther. The UN soldiers thought they would soon return home. South Koreans thought their country would soon be united. The Chinese government warned that it would enter the war if the Yalu River was crossed.

General MacArthur refused to believe the Chinese threat. In his mind, this was a great opportunity to permanently stop the spread of communism. To him, this war was bigger than just Korea; he wanted to finish off the Cold War once and for all. On November 20, 1950, he gave the order for all commanders "to drive forward with all speed." The Chinese could interpret this movement as the first step toward an invasion of their own country. They had given their warning and now the UN troops were moving toward the Yalu River with no intention of stopping.

Six days later, 200,000 well-equipped Chinese soldiers attacked the UN troops. Alarm spread through the world. China, with the world's largest population, had unlimited manpower at home. They were also allies with the Soviets, the world's other nuclear power.

As in a chess game, the players or soldiers waited while their next move was planned in Washington, DC. On the battlefield, the Chinese made strange attempts to "psyche out" the Americans. The Communists would play amplified records of old American music throughout the night. At the very least, the music kept the Americans from sleeping. But the Communists also hoped to make them homesick. They hoped hearing the music would make them lose their will to fight. Between this and the cold mountain winter, UN forces waited in misery.

In less than two months the Chinese army drove UN forces out of North Korea. Although many American troops knew little of why they were in Korea, they now had something to fight for —their lives. Even though the UN forces stopped and fought, Seoul, the capital of South Korea, soon fell to the Communists for a second time in January, 1951. After a great invasion through Inchon, the UN and U.S. war plan had fallen apart. Now they were up against a fresh enemy with unlimited manpower. The world stood still as each country carefully considered its next move.

In General MacArthur's view, the Chinese had

to be forced from Korea. The only way to do this was to cut off their supplies. This meant direct air attacks on mainland China. Everyone knew the war would then mushroom into a much greater conflict. It was the way to win the war — if the United States was willing to go all out to win it.

President Truman and his advisers studied MacArthur's plan. The general had all their respect. He had a distinguished record in World War I. MacArthur had commanded the forces that defeated Japan in World War II. He then governed occupied Japan in a manner that was widely praised. The landing at Inchon had made him a hero at home. Even with all that in mind, President Truman refused MacArthur's request. He felt certain that attacks on China would bring the Soviet Union into the war. This would bring on World War III, and the death of a large part of the human race due to atomic bombs.

MacArthur felt the United States had made a grave mistake. His displeasure found its way back to the United States. Everyone knew about his disagreement with the president. MacArthur's conduct brought about a crisis for the government. The general's opinions were needed for Truman to make a decision. But once the decision was made, many felt a soldier should not be seen disagreeing with his superior. President Truman came to the conclusion that MacArthur could no longer be an effective commander. He removed General MacArthur from his post. "I have concluded," Truman told America, "that . . . Mac-

General Douglas MacArthur

Arthur is unable to give his wholehearted support to the policies of the U.S. Government."

The United States was in shock. The general soon became the most popular man in America; while the president who dismissed him became a goat in many eyes. MacArthur was welcomed home with a great ticker-tape parade in New York City. In the next few years, Congress investigated the incident, and ruled that Truman had acted correctly. Historians also defend the President's actions.

General Matthew Ridgway took over as head of the UN forces, now composed of soldiers from sixteen countries. The Chinese and North Koreans immediately began a major attack to unite the Korean peninsula under communism. The UN forces held tough under the attack. The Communists realized that the war could never be won. Neither side wished the conflict to grow.

On June 23, 1951, the Soviet spokesman at the UN proposed a cease-fire that would end the war. But it was a long process. The fighting did not end for two more years. In America, more and more young men were drafted into the armed forces. Finally, an armistice, or peace treaty, was signed on July 27, 1953. President Dwight Eisenhower's announcement lacked the excitement of previous peace signings. "We have won an armistice on a battleground," he told the United States, "not peace in the world. We may not now relax our guard nor cease our quest." In essence, as long as communism existed, there would be no "peace," even if there was no particular battlefield.

The Inchon landing and the Inchon-Seoul offensive didn't turn the tide like other battles in this book. This great military maneuver would have brought a quick end to the Korean War but for the Chinese invasion. The Inchon landing had the same skill and luck that was involved in other great battles, but warfare had changed. There was no neat and tidy ending such as those at the close of the two world wars.

The Korean War was a new type of war, called "limited war." The war had begun with General MacArthur interested only in the same "total victory" found in previous wars. But with the lessons of other world wars, and the threat of nuclear war, things other than total victory also became important. Few battles were fought in this new type of war. Instead, the object was to hold your enemy in place, while waiting for diplomats to find a solution to the problem. Many times these solutions were only temporary.

The Korean War had been the only war to have both types of fighting. On this battlefield, a transition had been made in military history. This new idea of a "limited war" grew out of the Korean experience and still remains an important part of modern warfare.

Many Americans saw the Korean War as a wasted effort. North and South Korea continued to be separate — and more angry with one another than before the war. The cost of the war had had a grave impact on the American economy. And, of course, many Americans had been killed in action.

But the Communist invasion had been stopped. The democratic nations of the world had shown that they would not stand by and allow communism to be spread by military might. The UN had shown it could rally the world around a cause. Finally, Americans hoped, the United States had learned a lesson on how to prevent long, drawn-out conflicts.

Modern Warfare

The Korean War changed the way America viewed other countries and war. But this would not keep the United States from more drawn-out conflicts. There have been no attacks on the United States in the last thirty years. Instead, wars developed along the line set forward in Korea. Soldiers would still do the fighting but the politicians would control the war.

In this type of war, soldiers don't necessarily fight battles. They are involved in skirmishes while diplomats work to solve the problems. Soldiers still pull the triggers of their weapons, but only when given specific permission by the U.S. government. For this reason, there aren't any specific turning points in the Vietnamese and Persian Gulf wars.

Possibly the most important aspect of this new warfare was the role of the American public. In the past, the public had rarely questioned their leaders. If America was at war, it meant that every single American helped pay the price. But in situations like Korea, where the U.S. President made his own decision to enter the war, Americans felt less of a responsibility to support the cause. This diplomatic warfare was just as costly in life and property as other warfare. Yet, Americans had very little say in whether or not the fighting took place. Whereas views of the home front in the two world wars had been of Americans working and investing money to help the cause, now the home front was filled with confusion and disunity.

One reason for these disagreements was that Americans had access to more firsthand information about war. Americans received their information about the war in many ways. Beginning with the Vietnamese War, journalists accompanied American soldiers into war. The technology of radio and television allowed their reports to reach Americans almost immediately. The chilling, firsthand reports of warfare changed many American attitudes toward war.

Although the Vietnamese War was the first war reported mainly through radio and television, the Gulf War was the first "live" war. Many Americans could watch the war unfold on television news stations. Americans were being given enough information to make their own decisions about whether or not a war was right.

The Vietnamese War

After World War II, most European nations released their colonies in Africa and Asia. But France did not want to give up its oversea empire. Its colonies had been a great source of income. Now, they needed all the money they could get to rebuild their shattered country.

In one of these colonies, Vietnam, the Vietnamese formed a resistance movement. These rebels believed in a Communist form of government such as that of China, the Soviet Union, and North Korea. In September of 1945, these Communist believers set up their own country led by Ho Chi Minh, the Democratic Republic of Vietnam (DRV). A few months later, the French tried to regain Vietnam from the Communists. No one believed they would have any problem defeating the rebels. But these rebel forces knew the dense jungle and used it to their advantage. By using guerrilla warfare, the rebels decreased the importance of the huge number of French forces.

Ho Chi Min, President of North Vietnam

Guerrilla bands are small, compact fighting units that specialize in surprise hit-and-run attacks. Appearing suddenly, as if from nowhere, these rebels would shoot or knife half-a-dozen or more advancing French troops and then disappear into the underbrush. The surviving French troops would be terrified of the next attack. It was a way of fighting similar to the way Native Americans had fought different groups in North America.

The war with France dragged on for years. As French citizens at home lost patience, France decided to make one attempt to bring the rebels out of the jungle and into a conventional battle. They accomplished this, but miscalculated their enemy's strength. They found themselves stuck in a drawn-out battle, their troops trapped in the jungle. Now the French began looking elsewhere for help. Up till this point, the United States had supported the French effort with money and war supplies. French leaders asked the United States to begin air attacks — maybe even using an atomic bomb.

The United States had given the French support only because they were fighting a Communist enemy. The Soviet Union and China were supporting the Vietnamese rebels. If the United States attacked, these two nations might become involved. Doesn't this situation sound incredibly similar to the one you read about in the last chapter concerning Korea?

President Dwight Eisenhower refused the French request. Within days, the French troops had withdrawn and given up Vietnam. But now it was the United States that was having second thoughts about allowing Ho Chi Minh's forces to make this entire nation Communist. In an about-face that seemed to happen overnight, the United States began to offer massive support to those Vietnamese from the South who were fighting the takeover.

At an international peace conference following the French withdrawal, it was decided to divide Vietnam into a North and South. On either side of this dividing line there was to be a narrow demilitarized zone (DMZ) where no troops would be allowed. Ho Chi Minh's government was given control of the North. The United States began sending aid to South Vietnam, including hundreds of military advisers to train the Vietnamese. This presence continued to grow. By the end of President Eisenhower's term in office in 1961, there were more than 2,000 U.S. military advisers in South Vietnam.

Ho Chi Minh's forces, later to be known as Vietcong (Vietnamese Communists), began guerrilla raids into the South. When John F. Kennedy succeeded Eisenhower as president in 1961, he immediately sent the U.S. elite Special Forces, known as Green Berets, as combat advisers. He also sent a number of armed helicopters with American pilots. Within two years, the United States force grew to 15,000.

Since the United States was not officially at war with North Vietnam, the Green Berets were not supposed to fight the Vietcong. However, these American soldiers were involved in fighting as early as 1961. The American public was told that their troops were continuing training and intelligence work; the U.S. government did not want Americans to know that some of their troops were already engaged in fighting.

In the United States, Kennedy was assassinated on November 22, 1963. His successor, Lyndon B. Johnson, was a firm believer in the domino theory discussed during the Korean War. If Vietnam fell to communism, the whole of Southeast Asia could be lost. His first step was to order secret aerial bombing of North Vietnam.

Following a battle between Vietcong and U.S. Navy ships, Johnson had Congress pass the Tonkin Gulf Resolution in August, 1964. This was not a formal declaration of war, but it was closer to one than Truman ever had while fighting the Korean War. The resolution gave Johnson the authority "to take all necessary measures to repel any armed attack against the forces of the United States and to take all measures necessary, including the use of armed force, to assist South Vietnam." This would be the basis for the United States entering *the longest war in American history*.

By the end of 1964 there were nearly 25,000 American "advisers" in Vietnam. Finally, at the beginning of 1965, these troops were officially allowed to take part in combat against the Vietcong. Johnson and others felt that bombing civilian areas would break the people's will to fight. When they saw the great firepower they were up against,

President Lyndon B. Johnson presenting the Medal of Honor

the war could possibly end before it ever really started! The Americans were wrong — dead wrong.

These early bombing runs raised instead of lowered the people's will to fight. The war grew, and so did the U.S. commitment. By the end of 1965 there were over 200,000 U.S. combat troops in Vietnam. The Vietnamese War had become an American war. If you feel confused as to how and why this happened, so were many Americans at that time.

The 1960's were a time of turmoil and revolt in the United States. Teenagers questioned the authority of government, parents, and others. The Vietnamese War partially caused this revolt, as people began to feel that they couldn't trust their own government. Americans felt that their own government, for political reasons, would not tell them the truth. The war also gave these revolutionaries a cause: The groups began to band together and started what is known today as a "Peace Movement."

As reports of fighting in Vietnam grew, more and more Americans of all ages took to the streets asking how this had happened. Why hadn't they — or at least their Congressmen — been consulted? Who made the decision to go to war, after all?

In the early 1960's, college students were the ones asking these questions. They demanded answers, but found none. They held sit-ins for days at a time, and sometimes rioted. By 1965, antiwar protests involved many more people and had become commonplace all over America. Often, these protests would be attended by hundreds of thousands of Americans. The protests were held in many public places, but they were most often held on college campuses. One reason for this was the military draft that was forcing many young Americans to go to a war they neither understood nor believed in.

At the battlefront, soldiers got a sense of the lack of support for them at home. However, they had to be more concerned with survival. The fighting in Vietnam was different from anything Americans had ever seen, and they were caught unprepared. This was the first American "teenage" war: The average age of all the U.S. combat soldiers was barely 19 as opposed to 26 years of age in World War II! Most had just graduated or dropped out from high school. There was little unity in each military unit. Officers were often college graduates who had only served between six months and a year. Often, they were unable to form a bond with their troops. Many volunteer soldiers resented these officers who would soon leave the front.

But this was not the greatest enemy to American morale. Instead, the greatest blow to morale was the type of war that the Vietcong fought. The enemy refused to stand and fight any major battles. They filled the jungle with deadly booby traps. Trip wires were run across many trails to set off explosives. "Punji sticks," with razor-sharp pieces of bamboo could swing down from the trees at any moment. Often, the Americans would enter an innocent-looking village only to find it was a trap for ambush. Too often, the Americans were fighting an enemy they could neither identify nor see.

The constant fear caused by these battle tactics changed the face of the Vietnamese War. The morale of American soldiers was dismal. Often, they lashed out at innocent civilians. To protect themselves from ambush, many American troops set fire to any village in their path. Many learned to shoot first and ask questions later, and many resorted to battle tactics that are highly criticized today. One of these was the use of the chemical Agent Orange. This chemical caused the jungle plants to die, stripping the Vietcong of their hiding places. As a legacy of the war, this chemical permanently ruined much of the farmland in southern Vietnam. And American veterans who were infected by the chemical have contracted cancer and many other side-effects.

The Vietnamese War was the first time that American officers were forced to take strict body counts of the wounded and the dead. These grisly daily numbers hurt the soldiers' morale, as well as that of Americans receiving the news reports at home. In spite of these facts, the American leader, General William Westmoreland, slowly began to feel that his troops were close to winning the war. In January 1968, both sides agreed to stop fighting in order to observe a Vietnamese holiday, Tet. Instead, Ho Chi Minh mounted a great offensive against South Vietnam. The surprise of the Tet

Offensive shocked the world. It was a military failure but it succeeded in destroying America's will to continue the war.

After initial victories, the American forces drove the Vietcong back out of the South. By any military assessment, the United States had won the Tet Offensive: the Vietcong had lost 45,000 troops; the United States, 4,200. But the American public viewed this as a defeat. This was a bigger war than they had expected, and they refused to accept it anymore! The Tet Offensive acted to wake everyone up to the seriousness of the Vietnamese War. Johnson soon announced that he would not seek reelection. The pressure on him was more than he could bear. In November, 1968, Richard M. Nixon was elected President of the United States. He promised to end the draft and gradually bring home the American troops.

In actuality, Nixon widened the scope of the Vietnamese War by invading Cambodia and Laos. He also increased the bombing of North Vietnam. Like Johnson, Nixon had no intention of being the first American president to lose a war. But Congress and the American public grew more and more outraged. Whether responding to pressure or his own plan, Nixon began decreasing the number of Americans in Vietnam by relying more on South Vietnamese soldiers. In reality, this could only mean one thing: the loss of the war.

The Vietcong reacted with their strongest attack in the spring of 1972. The Americans repelled the attack, and Nixon ordered the heaviest air raids

President Richard M. Nixon greeting a GI in Vietnam

of the war. By 1973, the war had reached a stalemate. Peace talks began; on January 27, the Paris
Accords were signed. By spring, American forces
would return home. Immediately, both sides began violating the agreements. Nixon was in favor
of resuming the bombing, but America had had
enough. Congress passed the historic War Powers
Act, restricting any future military action without
their approval. The U.S. troops pulled out, leaving
South Vietnam open to Vietcong invasion. In essence, they had already won the war.

At home, the returning U.S. soldiers were not
welcomed. Americans were too busy dealing with
their own feelings about this war that seemed so
senseless, but on which they had spent $165 billion
and 58,000 lives. In the past, soldiers were always
welcomed home with great parades. The lack of
pride in the Vietnamese War emerged as many

A Vietnam veteran weeping at the Vietnam Veterans Memorial in Washington, D.C.

Americans blamed the returning soldiers for the war. This is one of the darkest times in U.S. history. Many of the soldiers returned, only to be outcasts from American society. It would take nearly fifteen years for America to realize what it had done to them. Only then were parades held and monuments erected. But the damage had already been done to many veterans of the war.

As of this writing, Vietnam exists today as one Communist nation. Millions of Vietnamese have fled to neighboring countries. In the United States, Americans slowly learned to call what went on in Vietnam a "war" and not a "conflict," as it was called for many years. Slowly, soldiers who participated in Vietnam have been recognized in memorials, including the famous one in Washington, DC.

Many of the veterans still hold a grudge against their nation and the war that changed their lives. But in recent years, many observers believe the United States has shown that it learned a valuable lesson in Vietnam. The United States would think long and hard before it ever again used military force to help carry out its diplomacy. And when that force was used, the United States learned that it must coordinate its armed forces for decisive fighting. Finally, the Vietnamese War showed once and for all how important the public's opinion had become. The public would not stand for secrecy and lying from its government. Public opinion had become more important than ever before.

The Persian Gulf War

The lessons of Vietnam have affected American policy in many ways. This was never more evident than, on August 2, 1990, when Iraqi troops rolled into their peaceful neighbor, Kuwait. They took it over and proclaimed it part of their own country. The world was shocked, but no one was quite sure whose responsibility it was to help the Kuwaitis.

Many countries criticized the invasion. The United Nations (UN) asked all its member countries not to trade with Iraq. Neighboring nations shut off access routes to Iraq. Iraq was isolated from the world by these embargoes, or restrictions, on trade. The UN also demanded that Iraq retreat from Kuwait and allow the previous leaders to return to power.

That didn't stop Iraqi President Saddam Hussein. On August 4, Hussein ordered his troops to gather along the border with Saudi Arabia. Saudi Arabia has the world's largest petroleum reserves.

Iraqi President Saddam Hussein

This is the oil that is transported throughout the world to fuel cars and factories in nearly every nation — particularly the United States. The United States and other nations decided trade sanctions were not enough — action was necessary.

"I ask for your support," U.S. President George Bush told the world on August 8, "in the decision . . . to stand up for what's right and condemn what's wrong, all in the cause of peace." It was bold action by the United States. But without world support, it would have never happened. "This will not be another Vietnam," Bush told Americans. Indeed, the United States was not alone as it had been in Vietnam. Troops and supplies from twenty-eight nations were sent to the region. Hussein would not be allowed to go any further. The UN was the gathering force behind this coalition of nations. Whether or not they agreed, many Americans wore yellow ribbons to show their support for the soldiers.

For years, Hussein had made other nations nervous. He had gathered the largest military in the Middle East: over one million troops, 5,000 tanks, missiles that could travel to other countries, and chemical weapons. In an eight-year war with Iran, from 1980 to 1988, he had shown himself to be a ruthless leader. He used illegal chemical weapons to burn the countryside and kill all human, animal, and plant life in his path. Hussein had even used these weapons against an entire Iraqi village whose occupants he suspected had helped the Iranians. His legacy of cruelty was compared by many to that of Adolf Hitler.

The long war with Iran had cost Iraq greatly, and it had been plunged into great debt. President Hussein ordered the Kuwaitis to lower their oil production so that oil prices would rise. He hoped this rise in oil prices would bring his nation, which produces a lot of oil, the money he needed. Kuwait refused. Hussein decided to use his powerful military to capture his wealthy neighbor. This move would lengthen Iraq's border on the Persian Gulf, which would allow for easier trade. It also gave Kuwait's rich oil fields to Iraq, and made Iraq a close second to Saudi Arabia in world oil reserves. But Hussein did not foresee the world's united interest in this area. Bush spoke for the world when he said, "the acquisition of land by force is unacceptable."

The world condemned Hussein's action. The UN Securities Council voted 14 to 0 (with Yemen abstaining) to demand his immediate withdrawal. Many of Iraq's Arab neighbors — whose support Hussein had been counting on — sided against him. Rarely do the world's powers agree on politics. But Iraq's action was so bold and threatening that it overcame many countries' differences.

For many years, Iraq had had a military relationship with the Soviet Union. Only a year earlier, this Gulf Crisis could have turned into an event such as Korea and Vietnam. But the Soviet Union was coming apart. People's confidence in communism was breaking. Soviet leaders had to concentrate all their efforts at home, not on international problems. The Soviets also no longer considered the United States its absolute enemy. They were no longer interested in automatically taking opposing views on issues against the United States. The invasion of Kuwait found the United States and Soviet Union on the same side of an issue for the first time since the Cold War had heated up during the Korean War.

"A line has been drawn in the sand," said President Bush. That line was the border of Saudi Arabia. If Hussein's troops crossed it, there would be war. It was this threat that caused Saudi Arabia to take the unheard of act of asking the United States for military protection. Without a strong military, the Saudis feared Hussein's troops would easily invade their nation.

Five months of standoff ensued. The UN made no bones about its feelings: Only a total withdrawal was acceptable. But Hussein refused. During these months, the defensive war planned around the "line in the sand" totally changed. Realizing that Hussein would not leave Kuwait, the UN was faced with the need to use force to drive the Iraqis out. The original plan, code-named "Operation Desert Shield," was altered to include an offensive campaign — "Operation Desert Storm" — that would force the Iraqis out of Kuwait. Hundreds of thousands of troops and the largest gathering of artillery since World War II took place during the next few months.

Realizing what he was up against, Hussein began using terrorism against his enemies. Hussein kept nearly 10,000 Americans and Europeans from leaving Iraq and placed them in locations he feared the coalition might bomb. He hoped they would act as "human shields" to prevent such bombing. During this period, many Iraqis and Kuwaitis saw that war was imminent. Nearly one million people fled Iraq and Kuwait, flooding neighboring nations, such as Jordan and Turkey.

Hussein saw only one way out of this situation — and it was not withdrawal. His pride would never allow him to withdraw his troops. He would try to widen the conflict. For years, Iraq and the other Arab nations that make up the Middle East had fought with their non-Arab neighbor, Israel. If Hussein could draw Israel into the war, he hoped his Arab neighbors would come to his aid. Arab leaders had made secret agreements to always support one another against Israel. This began one of the most horrifying memories in recent history.

Hussein ordered missiles, known as SCUDS, to be fired at Israel. You must remember that, up till this point, Israel had had no involvement in the conflict. People all over the world watched these attacks live on television. In major Israeli cities, the bomb-raid sirens would blare, while reporters and civilians donned gas masks and ran for bomb shelters. During the conflict, Hussein fired SCUDS at Israel and Saudi Arabia. Many of these missiles were intercepted by a piece of American technology, the Patriot missile. These missile systems used radar to track incoming SCUDS. Then they would take off and destroy the SCUDS before they reached the ground. But the Patriots could not catch every SCUD, and some got through and caused damage. In order to keep the war from growing, Israel restrained itself from attacking Iraq. Some experts say this restraint was the turning point of the Gulf War.

On November 29, the UN told Hussein that force would be used against Iraq if his troops did not withdraw by January 15, 1991. In December, Hussein allowed all foreigners to leave Iraq. During the next month, diplomats traveled the world trying to work out an agreement that would prevent war. It was to no avail. The deadline passed and the world waited as an international force of 680,000 troops — 415,000 of them Americans — awaited their instructions. For the first time in history, these fighting troops were not all men. The American forces in particular had women soldiers filling many roles.

January 16 is the day that few people in the world will ever forget. Again, television broadcast live the first attacks as American, British, French, Saudi, and Kuwaiti air forces began a crippling barrage of bombing. The war in the Persian Gulf had begun. "This is an historic moment," President Bush told the world. "I am convinced not only that we will prevail, but that out of the horror of combat will come the recognition that no nation can stand against a world united." Americans watched as U.S. planes flew over Baghdad, the Iraqi capital, and dropped thousands of bombs on Iraqi buildings and civilians.

The bombing used technology that few had ever dreamed possible. "Smart" bombs dropped from planes were programmed to destroy military buildings in Iraq, as well as factories and communication headquarters. Called surgical bombing, these attacks would destroy the programmed site while doing minimal damage to surrounding areas. Iraq's communications systems were quickly destroyed. Its air force could never get off the ground. The coalition pilots controlled the air from the word "GO"!

Life grew increasingly difficult in Iraq. The

bombing continued for over a month. With no water or electricity, everyday life was impossible. Bombing raids occurred around the clock. And many of the surgical bombs missed their targets and cost the lives of many Iraqis. Iraqis lived in constant fear, but still their leader would not relent. In fact, Hussein again threatened the world with terrorism. He claimed armies of terrorists had been sent throughout the world. Security at airports and public places worldwide was stepped up. And few Americans will forget the Super Bowl, which had some of the strictest security measures ever used at such a sporting event.

Instead of attacking the public, Hussein introduced a new form of terrorism termed "eco-terrorism." The Iraqis opened up Kuwaiti oil wells into the Persian Gulf, creating one of the largest oil spills in history. They hoped this would infect the drinking water in Saudi Arabia. Then they systematically set hundreds of Kuwaiti oil wells on fire. These well fires burn continuously as the flammable oil sprays out of the ground. They emit a thick black smoke that the troops hoped would shield them from the coalition air force. Instead, the smoke kept the sun from Kuwait for months, and created horrible air pollution in that entire region.

Toward the end of January, the bombing was directed to the Iraqi troops along the Saudi border. First, bridges and roads were destroyed. This left the troops with no supplies and little communication. These troops dug deeper into their fortifications and waited for the land attack that they knew would come soon.

In the United States, many Americans were stunned at how easy the war seemed to be. Others were more critical. They saw little reason for the United States to be helping Kuwait. But for the most part, Americans united behind their troops — this was the result of another lesson of Vietnam. However, politicians feared how the American people would react to a land attack. During such an attack, the well-secured Iraqis would wait for the coalition soldiers to come to them. Then, the Iraqis could use chemical weapons that would leave many soldiers dead. Once the casualties began to pile up, military planners feared the American public would lose its stomach for the war. They believed that this was what Hussein was waiting for.

Hussein continued to refuse to withdraw his troops. On February 23, soldiers from Kuwait, the United States, Britain, France, Egypt, and Saudi Arabia moved in with tanks and guns to drive the Iraqis out of Kuwait. Commander of the coalition forces General Norman Schwarzkopf referred to the plan as the "hail mary play in football." Military planners estimate that, under normal conditions, an attacking force should have a five-to-one ratio in personnel over their enemy. Although the coalition forces were outnumbered three to two, Schwarzkopf decided that to attack now was his army's best chance for a speedy victory.

By looking at satellite photographs, coalition

General H. Norman Schwarzkopf in Saudi Arabia

leaders could see that the Iraqi troops were gathered along the Persian Gulf coast expecting an amphibious attack. But this was not to be D day or Inchon. U.S. Marines came close to shore in order to make the Iraqis believe they were going to land on the beach. But the "hail mary" was taking place to their rear.

Troops from the U.S. and France drove hundreds of miles across the Iraqi desert at top speed to get around the Iraqi troops. When they reached the far side of Iraq, the Iraqis were surrounded before they even knew what had happened. "There is no way out," General Schwarzkopf told the world. "The gates are closed." Schwarzkopf would later explain, "At that point, coalition forces were only 150 miles from Baghdad. If our intention had been to totally defeat Iraq, there would have been nothing stopping them." But the coalition's only goal was to destroy Iraq's military and force them out of Kuwait.

Many of the Iraqi troops had been in the desert without food or water for days. The United States had dropped leaflets from planes telling them how to surrender, and assuring them that they would be treated well. But no one was prepared for the number of Iraqis that chose to do so. Hundreds of thousands of Iraqis surrendered within the first day of fighting. Huge camps had to be set up in Saudi Arabia to house them. The coalition troops were slowed as they took the time to destroy each of Iraq's tanks and other weapons. But there *was* fighting. "It is not a Nintendo game," explained Schwarzkopf. "It's a tough battlefield where people are risking their lives all the time."

But even Schwarzkopf was unprepared for how well the attack came off. Months of planning had made these armies from many nations act like a well-trained team. The general described it as "miraculous" that less than 200 U.S. soldiers lost their lives. The Iraqi losses were much heavier — estimated to be over 100,000. But in only 100 hours Kuwait had been freed. The Iraqis had not used any chemical weapons. In fact, many Iraqi troops hadn't put up any fight at all. Some even thanked the coalition for "rescuing" them from the desert.

On February 27, Kuwaiti forces were the first to drive into their capital and raise their nation's flag

General Colin Powell, Joint Chief of Staff during the Persian Gulf War

again. They thanked the world for its help and generosity. But this war had been for something greater than Kuwait's freedom. Communism's collapse in the Soviet Union had changed the face of world politics. With the United States and Soviet Union no longer at odds, the world could unite against wrongdoers. Through international cooperation, the UN could act as a world police force.

There were no battles in the Persian Gulf War such as those in World Wars I and II. The fighting was controlled by politicians as much as military leaders. Much like in Vietnam, some of the most important acts of the war occurred over diplomatic meeting tables. When fighting finally took place, it was carried off quickly and with little resistance from the Iraqis. War came only as a last resort. Possibly, this is the greatest lesson America has learned from its earlier wars, and from each of the great battles that decided them.

No one really knows how battles will be fought in the future. But most military analysts are convinced that the Gulf War illustrated the future of warfare. They foresee countries banding together against aggressors such as Saddam Hussein. Armies will be made more mobile than before. This will allow them to be moved quickly to areas such as the Middle East when they are needed. Even so, there will always be one common link between battles of the past, present, and future: the courage of the soldiers who are willing to put their lives on the line for something in which they believe.

War is a terrifying occurrence. It kills many people, damages countless other lives, harms the environment, and breeds more wars. Still, each of the great battles contained in this book had to be fought. And it was the courage of the soldiers that made each one a great point in American history. When asked why they were in the Middle East, American soldiers and their general gave the same response given by Americans in each of the battles you have read about: "Some things are worth fighting for."

Bibliography

Berger, Gilda. *Kuwait and the Rim of Arabia*. New York: Franklin Watts, 1978.

Bliven, Bruce, Jr. *The Story of D-Day*. New York: Random House, 1946.

Burke, Davis. *Black Heroes of the American Revolution*. New York: Harcourt, 1976.

Catton, Bruce. *The American Heritage Short History of the Civil War*. New York: Dell, 1963.

———. *The Battle of Gettysburg*. New York: Harper and Row, 1963.

Chaikin, Miriam. *A Nightmare in History: The Holocaust, 1933–1945*. New York: Clarion Books, 1987.

Clark, Clorinda. *The American Revolution, 1775–1783: A British View*. New York: McGraw, 1967.

Cook, Fred. *The Golden Book of the American Revolution*. New York: Golden Press, 1959.

Dank, Milton. *D-Day*. New York: Franklin Watts, 1984.

Dawidowicz, Lucy S. *War Against the Jews: 1933–1945*. New York: Holt, Rinehart & Winston, 1975.

Dupuy, R. Ernes, and Trevor N. Dupuy. *Encyclopedia of Military History*. New York: Harper & Row, 1986.

Ellis, David Maldwyn. *The Saratoga Campaign*. New York: McGraw-Hill, 1969.

Fincher, E.B. *The Vietnam War*. New York: Franklin Watts, 1980.

———. *The War in Korea*. New York: Franklin Watts, 1981.

Gilbert, Martin. *The Second World War*. New York: Henry Holt & Co., 1989.

Goldston, Robert. *The Causes of the Civil War*. New York: Macmillan, 1972.

Hastings, Max. *The Korean War*. New York: Simon & Schuster, 1987.

Hilberg, Raul. *The Destruction of the European Jews*. New York: Harper & Row, 1961.

Hoobler, Dorothy and Thomas. *The Trenches*. New York: G.P. Putnam's Sons, 1979.

Karnow, Stanley. *Vietnam: A History*. New York: Viking Press, 1983.

Katz, William Loren. *An Album of the Civil War*. New York: Franklin Watts, 1974.

Langley, Michael. *Inchon Landing*. New York: Times Books, 1979.

Lawson, Dan. *The U.S. in the Spanish-American War*. New York: Albert-Schumann, 1976.

Lens, Sidney. *Vietnam: A War on Two Fronts*. New York: Lodestar, 1990.

Marrin, Albert. *The Spanish-American War*. New York: Atheneum, 1991.

McPherson, James M. *Marching Toward Freedom*. New York: Knopf, 1965.

Mercer, Charles. *Miracle at Midway*. New York: G.P. Putnam & Sons, 1977.

Messenger, Charles. *The Second World War*. New York: Franklin Watts, 1987.

Parkinson, Roger. *Origins of World War One*. East Sussex, England: Wayland Ltd., 1977.

———. *The Origins of World War Two*. East Sussex, England: Wayland Ltd., 1980.

Reeder, Colonel Red. *The Story of the Spanish-American War*. New York: Duell, Sloan and Pearce, 1966.

Ribbons, Ian. *Battle of Gettysburg*. London: Oxford University Press, 1974.

———. *Tuesday 4 August, 1914*. New York: David White, Inc., 1970.

Webster's American Military Biographies. Springfield, MA: G&C Merriam Company, Publishers, 1978.

Yass, Marion. *Hiroshima*. East Sussex, England: Wayland Ltd., 1976.

Index

Page numbers for illustrations are in italics.

About the Author

Brian Black is currently finishing up graduate study in American studies. He was Associate Editor for *Scholastic News* for three years. He has written about history for various magazines and textbooks, including Scholastic's *American Adventures*. Currently, Brian, his wife, and two cats have found a home where the buffalo no longer roam in northeast Kansas.